THE TRUTH

About an Untruthful, Corrupt, Biased Decision made by Mr. Peter Millman a government Inspector, appointed by Secretary of State DEFRA. To preside over a Non-Statutory Public Inquiry 15, 16, 17th. September 2015, in Bedfordshire because a previous decision by an Inspector Mark Yates was quashed; because he failed to consider and evaluate all evidence made available to him at a Public Inquiry dated September 2013.
The Inquiry was an appeal under Section 53(5) and paragraph.4(1) of Schedule 14 of the Wildlife and Countryside Act 1981
The Inquiry was Videoed and Recorded.
also, a
Report of Events whilst dealing with
WOODFINE'S (SOLICITOR) BEDFORD
By Alan Bowers

Published by New Generation Publishing in 2021

Copyright © Alan Bowers 2021

First Edition

ISBN

Paperback	978-1-80031-170-1
Ebook	978-1-80031-169-5

www.newgeneration-publishing.com

New Generation Publishing

INDEX TO THE TRUTH

THE TRUTH:

CHAPTER: I

Details of the UNTRUTHFUL Public Inquiry decision by a Government Inspector.

THE TRUTH!

This document is a review of the proceedings and actions which occurred at a Non- Statutory Public Inquiry held September 2015, the reason for the Inquiry was because a previous inquiry and decision by a previous Inspector (Mark Yates September 2013) was quashed because it failed to consider and evaluate all evidence made available to the inquiry.

The Inquiry was to be a three day Inquiry but was concluded after one and a half days.

This review is based upon actual facts as filmed and recorded; and information found in the decision letter issued by the Inspector who presided (Mr. Peter Millman).

The proceedings were filmed and recorded at the request and cost by Mr Alan Bowers. The reason for the request was because of the mistrust Mr. Bowers and others had experienced while attending previous Public Inquiries concerning Rights of Way. It should be noted that Central Bedfordshire Council objected to having the proceedings filmed but they were overruled.

The Inquiry was made under "Section 53 (5) and paragraph 4 (1) of the schedule 14 of the Wildlife and Countryside Act 1981" against the decision of Central Bedfordshire Council (The council) not to make an Order under section 53 (2) of that act.

The Council had Employed the services of a London based Barrister, in addition to, Rights of way officer of Central

Beds. Council; a locum solicitor; and various representatives of "Rights of Way" Groups.

Mr. Bowers represented himself assisted by Mr: Richard Connaughton and Mrs. Marlene Masters both of whom had suffered the injustice of "Rights of Way" issues.

At the very beginning of the Inquiry Mr. Millman (Inspector) informed the Inquiry that he would not allow Mr. Bowers to read out his opening statement or witness statements because *(Quote) "I am not prepared to waste the time of this Inquiry listening to material which cannot be relevant to My decision"* because of objections from various people attending the Inquiry, Mr Millman stated (Quote)

"This Inquiry is not about -what has happened since 1997: it cannot be relevant to what happened in 1997, because it occurred after 1997", he went on to say (Quote) *"I will accept the statements as read so that the council could concentrate on the relevant material in cross examination".* After further objections, he went on to say *"The material contained in the statement cannot be my concern by law; I cannot and will not consider the contents of the witness statements to be read out by law".*

Note! The Inquiry was scheduled to last 3 days; these proceedings were at the beginning of the first day.

The Inspector also refused Mr. Connaughton from questioning certain Council officials. Note! The Inspector had been in possession of Mr. Bowers witness statement many months before the Inquiry.

....

The filming of the one-and-a-half-day Inquiry has been divided into various sections for ease of access.

The Inspector did not allow Mr. Bowers to deliver his

opening statement and witness statement because it would be a waste of Inquiry time and was irrelevant to the case; he also denied Mr. Connaughton the opportunity to read his statement and to question Council officials.

On examination of the film, it can be seen that the Inspector allowed the Barrister a very long period (over one and a half hours) (Section 7,8,9 10 of the film) to question Mr. Bowers regarding information the Inspector had previously stated was irrelevant to the case. Although this was brought to the attention of the Inspector, he continued to allow the Barrister to continue.

The Barrister also tried to question the contents of new evidence (In the form of analysis of User Evidence) which the Inspector states in Paragraph 17 of his decision letter *(it cannot be considered new evidence. The Analysis also contains no new relevant evidence).* The Barrister was accused by members attending the Inquiry of "Clutching at Straws". Mr. Millman said "*I will decide who is Clutching at Straws".* It should be noted; that the Inspector had previously announced he would consider the presentation of Analysis of "User evidence forms" as new evidence.

When considering the contents of the Inspectors decision letter dated 2nd. October 2015: and the true evidence contained in the film it can be seen from the attitude and actions of the Inspector he was determined to refuse the Appeal.

On reflection, it was a wise decision to film and record the proceedings.

Signed A. J. Bowers   Dated 28th. January 2019.

CHAPTER: II

APPEAL DECISION:

Copy of Appeal decision Ref: FPS/P0420/14A/1R dated2nd. October 2015
Issued by Government Inspector Peter Millman.

Appeal Decision

Inquiry opened on 15 September 2015

by Peter Millman BA

an Inspector directed by the Secretary of State for Environment, Food and Rural Affairs

Decision date: 0 2 OCT 2015

Appeal Ref: FPS/P0420/14A/1R

- This Appeal is made under Section 53 (5) and Paragraph 4 (1) of Schedule 14 of the Wildlife and Countryside Act 1981 ("the 1981 Act") against the decision of Central Bedfordshire Council ("the Council") not to make an Order under section 53 (2) of that Act.
- The Application dated October 2008 was refused by the Council in February 2013.
- The Appellant, Mr A Bowers, claims that the Definitive Map and Statement of Public Rights of Way should be modified by deleting from it public footpath 28 in Maulden.

Summary of Decision: The Appeal is refused.

Preliminary Matters

1. I have been directed by the Secretary of State for Environment, Food and Rural Affairs to re-determine an Appeal under Section 53 (5) and Paragraph 4 (1) of Schedule 14 of the 1981 Act (see paragraph 4 below). This type of appeal is usually dealt with by means of written representations. Very occasionally a non-statutory inquiry is held. This was one of those occasions. The proceedings at the inquiry were recorded and filmed for Mr Bowers.

2. Mr Bowers was assisted at the inquiry by two principal advisers, neither of whom had formal legal qualifications. I saw it therefore as my responsibility to ensure, as far as possible, that Mr Bowers was not disadvantaged merely because he did not have recourse to formal legal advice. I made it clear in my opening remarks that I could not assist Mr Bowers to make out his case, but that if at any time he was unclear as to what was required of him, or if he was confused about procedure, he should ask me for advice, and that as long as it did not advance his case or prejudice the case of objectors, I would advise him and, if he wished, he could heed that advice. I also stated that I would alert Mr Bowers, where I considered it appropriate, if it became clear to me that he was concentrating on material that could have no effect on the outcome of the inquiry.

Background

3. Footpath 28 in Maulden runs northwards for about 100 metres from Clophill Road at Hall End to join bridleway 24 shortly before it enters Maulden Wood. It is a narrow path which runs between the appellant's property and a neighbouring house, but it is on the appellant's land. Between 1946 and the 1980s the land was used as a market garden. Footpath 28 was not shown on Bedfordshire County Council's Definitive Map when it was first compiled in the

1950s, although for reasons now unknown it was recorded in the Definitive Statement. An application was made by Mrs H Izzard to Bedfordshire County Council in 1992 to add the route to the Definitive Map as a footpath. The County Council made an order in 1995, to which there was one objection, from Mr A Bowers, the appellant. Because of the objection the order was submitted to the Secretary of State. It was confirmed by an inspector in 1997 on the basis of written representations and an accompanied site visit, and no inquiry or hearing was held. The appellant states that his legal advisers at the time, Messrs Molyneux Lucas, advised him to agree to the written representations procedure.

4. In 2008 Mr Bowers made an application for an order to delete the path from the Definitive Map, following unsuccessful attempts to extinguish it under the Highways Act 1980. The Council refused the application in 2013. Mr Bowers appealed against that refusal to the Secretary of State. The Secretary of State appointed an inspector to consider the appeal. The inspector decided that it should be refused. Mr Bowers applied for judicial review of that decision, and was successful. The decision was quashed on the grounds that the Inspector who considered the appeal erred in law when he refused to hear evidence which had not been considered by the Council Committee which decided to refuse Mr Bowers' application in 2013. The appeal must now be re-determined.

5. A non-statutory inquiry into Mr Bowers' appeal was to have been held in January 2015, but at the last minute the inspector directed to hold it became unavailable for personal reasons. The inquiry was therefore rescheduled for September 2015.

The Main Issues

6. Section 53(3)(c)(iii) of the 1981 Act provides that an order to modify the definitive map and statement must be made following the discovery of evidence which (when considered with all other relevant evidence available) shows that there is no public right of way over land shown in the map and statement as a highway of any description.

7. In the case of *Trevelyan v Secretary of State for Environment, Transport and the Regions* [2001], Lord Phillips MR held that: *Where the Secretary of State or an inspector appointed by him has to consider whether a right of way that Is marked on a definitive map in fact exists, he must start with an initial presumption that it does. If there were no evidence which made it reasonably arguable that such a right of way existed, it should not have been marked on the map. In the absence of evidence to the contrary, it should be assumed that the proper procedures were followed and thus that such evidence existed. At the end of the day, when all the evidence has been considered, the standard of proof required to justify a finding that no right of way exists is no more than the balance of probabilities. But evidence of some substance must be put In the balance, if it is to outweigh the initial presumption that the right of way exists. Proof of a negative is seldom easy, and the more time that elapses, the more difficult will be the task of adducing the positive evidence that is necessary to establish that a right of way that has been marked on a definitive map has been marked there by mistake.*

8. In *Trevelyan* the Court also quoted with approval guidance which had been published in Department of the Environment Circular 18/90. The guidance stated that it was for those who contended that there was no right of way to

prove that the definitive map was in error and that a mistake had been made when the right of way was first recorded; it also stated that the evidence needed to remove a right of way from the record would need to be cogent, and that it was not for the surveying authority to demonstrate that the map was correct.

9. Circular 18/90 has been superseded by Defra Circular 01/09. Circular 01/09 states at paragraph 4.33 *The evidence needed to remove what is shown as a public right from such an authoritative record as the definitive map and statement - and this would equally apply to the downgrading of a way with "higher" rights to a way with "lower" rights, as well as complete deletion - will need to fulfil certain stringent requirements. These are that:*

  • *the evidence must be new - an order to remove a right of way cannot be founded simply on the re-examination of evidence known at the time the definitive map was surveyed and made.*

  • *The evidence must be of sufficient substance to displace the presumption that the definitive map is correct.*

  • *The evidence must be cogent.*

10. The principal issues therefore are whether any new evidence has been produced and, if so, whether, when considered with all other relevant evidence, it shows on the balance of probabilities that there is no public right of way over footpath 28 and that an Order should be made to delete it from the Definitive Map and Statement.

Whether any new evidence has been produced

11. The decision to confirm the order adding footpath 28 to the Definitive Map in 1997 was based primarily on evidence of the use of the route by people the inspector considered were members of the public. The inspector, Rear Admiral Holley, decided that this evidence satisfied the test in s31 of the Highways Act 1980: *(1) Where a way over any land... has been actually enjoyed by the public as of right and without interruption for a full period of 20 years, the way is to be deemed to have been dedicated as a highway unless there is sufficient evidence that there was no intention during that period to dedicate it. (2) The period of 20 years referred to in subsection (1) above is to be calculated retrospectively from the date when the right of the public to use the way is brought into question...*

12. Inspector Holley found that the test was satisfied with respect to two separate 20 year periods. The first ended in 1956 when the route was obstructed for a short time, bringing the right of the public to use it into question. The second 20 year period ended in 1992 when the appellant blocked the route. The evidence considered included completed user evidence forms and records of interviews carried out by Council officers.

13. The Council accepts that new evidence, in the form of statements from local people, provided by the appellant in connection with his 2008 application for an order to delete footpath 28, shows that the statutory test for deemed dedication (paragraph 11 above) was not met for the period ending in 1992. What is at issue, therefore, is whether new evidence has been produced in relation to the earlier period between 1936 and 1956.

14. Mr Bowers argued that a letter written in 1957 by the County Surveyor to Mrs Izzard, the applicant for the 1995 order, (see below at paragraph 28) should be regarded as new evidence. It was not considered by the Committee which decided in 1995 to make the order, but it was, however, before Inspector Holley in 1997. It seems to me that 'new evidence' can only be evidence which was not before the ultimate decision maker, the Inspector. In a letter to the Development Management Committee of the Council dated 20 April 2013 Mr Bowers also referred to 'new evidence': *in the form of letters illustrating the collusion and impartiality* [sic] *of Rights of Way Officers when they presented their case to the meeting of members held 19 July 1995.* I have seen no evidence that relevant information was withheld from Inspector Holley in 1997.

15. When Inspector Holley considered user evidence in 1997, he noted at paragraph 11 of his Decision Letter in reporting the County Council's case: *A table has been drawn up to illustrate the years of claimed use; 13 of the users are related, some distantly, to the Applicant.* The Council produced, at the 2015 inquiry, a table, said to have been produced before the 1997 inquiry and possibly before the Committee meeting in 1995. It lists those who had given evidence of use. Beneath the column in the table headed 'Relationship to H Izzard', which shows the relationship of some users to the applicant for the order, whose family owned the land over which the footpath ran from 1936 to 1946, is the figure '13'. In my view it is likely that Inspector Holley took his figure of 13 from this table.

16. Mr Bowers argues that there has been a new analysis of the user evidence, and new information about the relationships of users to Mrs Izzard, which casts doubt on Inspector Holley's conclusions. He produced a chart at the inquiry, and in the evidence of one of his advisers, Mr R Connaughton, is a document headed *Analysis of user evidence forms submitted to Rights of Way officers presented to Committee members, 19 July 1995. Period to be considered 1935-1956.* Both these documents showed, they argued, that none of the user evidence considered by Inspector Holley was valid.

17. Counsel for the Council took Mr Bowers through his chart in great detail in cross-examination, comparing it with the 1995 table. In my view the cross-examination revealed that the evidence contained in the chart was essentially the same as that considered by the Inspector in 1997. It cannot be considered new evidence. The *Analysis* also contains no new relevant evidence.

18. I noted above at paragraph 13 that Mr Bowers' production of statements about footpath 28 persuaded the Council that the test for deemed dedication was not met for the period 1972 to 1992. Seventeen people provided information and the Council carried out additional telephone interviews with some of them. It was clear that this was new evidence, not before Inspector Holley in 1995.

19. Although this evidence only persuaded the Council to change its view of the later, 1972 to 1992, period, some relates to the earlier period of 1936 to 1956. Much of this is of minimal use in relation to that period; one person, for example, whose age was not stated, wrote that as a child she always walked along the nearby bridleway 'as footpath 28 did not exist.' Two of the seventeen people, however, had lived in Maulden from the 1930s. One had lived there since 1934 and stated that he did not walk the path and that the ' owner between 1946 and 1956 said it was not public. Another, who had lived there from 1937 to 1960, stated that he 'would not dream' of walking up the

appeal route. He stated further, 'It was only a track to the allotments, not a public footpath.'

20. The evidence considered in the previous paragraph is new. On its own it is far from cogent, and certainly would not outweigh the initial presumption that public footpath rights exist over footpath 28. But I now consider it in the light of the evidence available to Inspector Holley in 1997, bearing in mind, as noted by Andrew Nicql QC in *Burrows v Secretary of State* [2004], that an Inquiry: *cannot simply re-examine the same evidence that had previously been considered when the definitive map was previously drawn up. The new evidence has to be considered in the context of the evidence previously given, but there must be some new evidence which in combination with the previous evidence justifies a modification.*

Whether, when considered with all other relevant evidence, the new evidence is cogent and of sufficient substance to displace the presumption that the right of way exists

21. Although there is no new evidence of significance about those who stated that they had used the appeal route from 1936 to 1956, Mr Bowers and his advisers attacked Inspector Holley's conclusions about the user evidence on a number of grounds.

22. It was argued that the Inspector should have completely discounted the evidence of users who had not used the route throughout the 20 year period. If someone had walked the route for only 19 years, for example, his or her user evidence was invalid. Mr Bowers appeared to concede at the inquiry that this argument showed a misunderstanding of the law.

23. Mr Bowers also argued that Inspector Holley should have discounted a large amount of the use because users were family, friends and neighbours of the applicant for the 1995 order, whose family owned the land over which the appeal route ran from 1936 to 1946. Their use, it was argued, would not have been 'as of right' (paragraph 11 above); it would have been by permission or by a private right.

24. It is clear from his Decision Letter that Inspector Holley considered the relationship of users to the applicant's family in concluding that: *there is evidence from many other users who have not been shown to be other than members of the public.* In any event, no significant evidence was produced to the 2015 inquiry which suggested that permission was granted by a landowner between 1936 to 1956 to any person to use the path or that any private rights were granted or claimed.

25. Mr Bowers argued further that the users could not represent the public as a whole; they were a clearly defined part of it. His advisers referred to the judgment in *Poole v Huskinson* (1843), in which it was stated that there could not be a dedication to a limited part of the public. It is clear, however, that the law does not require a cross-section of users from the whole country to walk a path for dedication to the public to be deemed or implied. It is equally obvious that in a small hamlet such as Hall End would have been before 1956, with no wider attraction as a tourist destination, the great bulk of the users of local footpaths would have been local people. That does not mean that they are not representative of'the public.'

26. Mr Bowers expressed his regret that he had chosen not to exercise his right to be heard at a public inquiry in 1997 (paragraph 3 above). I accept that the weight to be given to user evidence untested by cross-examination at a public inquiry may not carry as much weight as evidence which has been tested and which has stood up successfully to that testing. Nevertheless the new evidence referred to in paragraph 19 above, considered with the matters referred to in the preceding five paragraphs, is insufficient to lead to a conclusion that the user evidence considered by Inspector Holley in 1997 needs re-evaluation.

27. I consider finally other attacks on Inspector Holley's decision, mounted by Mr Bowers' advisers but not said to involve new evidence. I noted above at paragraph 14 a letter written to Mrs Izzard, the applicant for the 1995 order, in 1957.- It read as follows: *Dear Madam, With reference to the interview you had with my assistant on Friday last, I enclose herewith a map showing the route of the public path* [this is agreed to have referred to the bridleway into which the appeal route runs (paragraph 3 above)]. *The broken red line indicates the occupation way* [now footpath 28], *which of course, is not a public path and therefore is not shown on the Draft Survey Map.* Inspector Holley considered that letter, but his conclusions are attacked on a number of grounds.

28. First it was argued that if a route is an occupation way it cannot be a public right of way. In my view that argument is based on a misunderstanding of the law; an occupation way which carries no additional rights will be private, but public use of such a path which satisfies the test in s31 of the Highways Act 1980 (paragraph 11 above) will, subject to the proviso about evidence of a lack of intention to dedicate, be deemed to have been dedicated to the public.

29. It was argued by Mrs M Masters, another of Mr Bowers' advisers, that when the County Surveyor told Mrs Izzard that the appeal route was not a public right of way, it must be presumed that he carried out a thorough investigation of all the then available evidence relating to the route. It must be presumed that everything that should have been done, she argued, was done properly. This is, it seems to me, intended to be an expression of the presumption of regularity. Mr Connaughton put it a different way. He argued that the County Surveyor would not have made the statement he did 'without the truth to back it. ' I do not accept these arguments; the presumption is that acts will have been carried out lawfully, not that whoever carried them out will have had knowledge of all relevant facts and will have come to the correct conclusion.

30. Mrs Masters also argued, on the same basis, that because the original Definitive Map for Bedfordshire did not show what became footpath 28, and because it must be presumed that those who compiled it carried out their investigations correctly, this was strong evidence that no public rights existed over the route. I reject that argument for the same reason that I reject Mrs Masters' argument about the County Surveyor's letter.

31. Mr Connaughton argued that, had the appeal route carried public rights, the fact would have shown up in the conveyance when the land was sold in 1946. That is, in my view, an assertion without evidential foundation.

32. Mr Connaughton also argued that all people 'of sound mind' would recognize the logic that no owner of a market garden (such as the owner of the land crossed by the appeal route from 1946 to 1956) who sold his produce to local people would allow the public to cross his land. That is not an argument based, as far as this route is concerned, on evidence.

33. Mr Connaughton noted the conclusion of the Inspector whose decision was quashed (paragraph 4 above) that the appeal route was not a 'designated right of way prior to 1997'. It followed, he argued, that it was therefore not a public right of way in 1956. It is clear to me that the Inspector's statement indicated nothing more than that the appeal route was not included in the Definitive Map and Statement prior to 1997.

34. Both Mr Connaughton and Mrs Masters argued, for various additional reasons, that owners of the land crossed by the path between 1936 and 1956 could not and would not have dedicated public rights of way across it. It seems to me that these arguments miss the fundamental point that to satisfy the test in s31 of the Highways Act 1980 (paragraph 11 above) actual dedication does not need to be proved. Upon the satisfaction of the test, dedication is **deemed** to have occurred, in other words, the effect of qualifying use of the route is the same as if dedication had actually occurred.

35. I conclude that the new evidence, considered together with all existing relevant evidence, is not cogent, and falls far short of displacing the presumption that the Definitive Map is correct in depicting footpath 28.

Conclusion

36. Having regard to these and all other matters raised at the inquiry and in the written representations I conclude that the Appeal should be refused.

Other matters

37. At the inquiry there was an attempt to air grievances about the conduct of the Council and its predecessors, as well as allegations about widespread malpractice within local authorities, the Planning Inspectorate and Defra. I made it clear that I could hear no such grievances and allegations or make any findings in connection with them.

Formal decision

38. *I* refuse the Appeal.

(peter Mitfman

Inspector

10

APPEARANCES

For Central Bedfordshire Council

Mr G Mackenzie   Of Counsel

He called:

Mr A Maciejewski   Senior Definitive Map Officer

Other objectors to the appeal

Mrs S Rumfitt   Of Sue Rumfitt Associates, representing the Open Spaces Society

For the appellant

Mr A Bowers   The appellant

He represented himself.
assisted by:

Mr R Connaughton
Mrs. M. Masters •

Supporter of the appeal

Mr B Hones

Interested party.

Mr M Westley   Of the East Herts Footpath Society

11

Documents handed in at inquiry

1. Mrs Masters' statement
2. Mr Bowers' opening and statement
3. Mr Bowers' chart and analysis of user evidence
4. Additional page re Mr Lockey
5. Mr Hones' documents
6. Mr Westley's submissions
7. Handwritten copy of Mrs Masters' cross-examination questions
8. Mrs Rumfitt's submissions
9. Mr Mackenzie's submissions
10. Mrs Masters' final submissions
11. Mr Connaughton's closing submission

CHAPTER: III

PROCEEDINGS:

**Details of proceedings which took place at Public Inquiry
Ref: FPS/P0420/1R on 15th-16th September 2015**

**PUBLIC INQUIRY HELD 15th – 16th, September 2015
To appeal against the
DECISION of CENTRAL BEDFORDSHIRE
COUNCIL NOT TO MAKE AN ORDER TO DELETE
FOOTPATH 28 IN MAULDEN BEDFORDSHIRE**

PROCEEDINGS:

After the primary statements had been made, Mr. Millman proceeded to inform the Public the purpose of the Public Inquiry.

He also stated that he was aware of the "Quality of Arms" of the situation, insomuch that the "Council" had instructed a Barrister to present their case at the very last moment; and that Mr. Bowers had no legally qualified support. He stated that it was his responsibility to ensure, as far as was possible to see that Mr. Bowers was not disadvantaged.

Mr. Millman referred to the Witness statement Mr. Bowers had presented to the Inspectorate. He informed the public that "He was not prepared to waste the time of the Inquiry to allow Mr. Bowers to read his statement because, it was <u>TOO</u> long and that most of the contents were not relevant to the case". Mr. Bowers raised an objection, stating that if it was not read out the members of the public would not be   aware of the events leading up to this Inquiry. Objections were also made by members of the public. Mr. Millman stated that [Quote] "I am not prepared to waste the time of this Inquiry listening to material which cannot be relevant to **MY** decision". After objections from Mr. Bowers and other people present. Mr. Millman stated [Quote]. "This inquiry is not about what has happened since 1997; it cannot be relevant to what happened in 1997, because it occurred after 1997". **NOTE! This Inquiry is about an appeal Ref: FPS/P0420/14R/1R against the decision of Central Bedfordshire Council dated 13th. February 2013 not to make an order under section 53 (2) of that act.** He went on to say [Quote] He would accept the statements as read, so that the council could concentrate on the relevant material in cross examination". It should be noted that there was no cross examination by the Council regarding the contents of Mr. Bowers statements. Mr. Bowers asked the Inspector if he (The Inspector) was concerned about the conduct and actions of the "Council". Mr. Millman informed Mr. Bowers that [Quote] "The material contained in the statement cannot be my concern by **LAW.**" He went on to say "I cannot and will not consider the contents of the witness statements to be read out by **LAW**". He therefore banned Mr. Bowers from reading and presenting his statement, saying that the Inspectorate and Council were aware of its contents and **he** considered it as read. The Inspector (Mr. Millman former Rights of Way Officer) also informed Mr. Bowers and others that; [Quote] "Any form of Misconduct or Malfeasance on behalf of the "Council" should be considered through other avenues, or court proceedings, referring to criminal proceedings "Misconduct in Public Office".

This also applied to the opening statement prepared by Mr. Bowers. In spite of objections from various people present Mr. Millman would not allow the statements to be heard by members of the public present at the Inquiry.

It should be noted that the Inquiry was due to last 3 days, the witness statement and Opening statements by Mr. Bowers were to be presented at the beginning of the Inquiry and that there was ample time to have heard both. The Inquiry finished after 2 days!

In the early stages of the Inquiry Mr. Millman made reference to a document concerning Mrs. Debbie Wiseman who is also a Rights of Way Victim in Suffolk. Mr. Millman states [Quote] "I received this document a few days ago, (he did not state where from). I have looked at it, and it could be seen as relevant to this case". He went on to ask the Council representative (Mr. Maciejewski) if there were copying facilities available. Which, indicated, he wished to distribute the document to people attending the Inquiry. Mrs. Masters informed Mr. Millman that the document he was referring to was not relevant to this Inquiry. Mr. Millman appeared to be confused and stated [Quote]. "I will leave it here on my desk for anyone to see". This document was not relevant evidence to the Inquiry and should not have been produced! I believe the Inspector was deliberately attempting to misdirect all those attending the Inquiry, and his actions were completely out of order.

It should also be noted that much time was allocated to the Barrister (30 minutes of irrelevant statements concerning non-users, which had already been deemed irrelevant), and other Rights of Way users (Open Spaces Society and East Herts. Footpath Society).

Mr. Millman decided that most of the evidence Mr. Bowers intended to present to the Public at the Inquiry, was [Quote] "In **his** view was irrelevant to the case" **All the evidence within Mr. Bowers statements and questions to the "Council" was Relevant!...**
  The information and documents contained in Mr. Bowers

statements indicated the Reluctance, and Determination of the "Council" to ensure Mr. Bowers would not be successful in Deleting the path.

The Public attending the Inquiry should have been made aware of the **fact** that the Elected Members of the "Council" wished the path to be removed. However, the "Council" were aware that if the path was **Deleted,** it would indicate that a mistake had been made in the first instance. The "Council" were also aware that if the path was **Deleted** they would be subject to paying compensation and reputational risks.

During the course of the Inquiry, the Inspector also banned Mr. Connaughton from asking the "Council" certain questions which would also have revealed, the determination of the "Council" to ensure that Footpath 28 would not be **Deleted,** for the same reasons stated above...The Inspector (Mr. Millman Former Rights of Way Officer) said [Quote} "It is not my job to look back at the way the council made its decision. I am looking at evidence relevant to what happened in 1997. I am not sure that this line of questioning will help me come to my decision".

In studying the video of the Inquiry, it can be seen that the Inspector (Mr. Millman) showed periods of Irritation and Frustration. At one point, when Mr. Maciejewski (Council Officer) was being questioned by Mr. Connaughton, the officer appeared uneasy and unable to respond to questions asked by Mr. Connaughton he appeared to claim the attention of the Inspector for guidance. The Inspector said "Do not look at me for assistance because I am not going to give you any" Although he did appear to attempt to lessen the impact of questions asked by Mr. Connaughton.

It should be noted that this Inquiry **WAS** about the decision made by the council 13th. February 2013. The previous decision made by Mr. Mark Yates **IPROW** was **Quashed** because he did not consider evidence made available after 1997!

We will now consider Evidence that the Inspector considered Relevant!

During the course of the Inquiry the contents of a letter issued by the County Surveyor, in 1957 was considered. This was evidence which was withheld from the decision-making committee in 1995, and was considered by the "Council" as "Of little value".

The Barrister for the "Council" tried to infer that the information contained within the letter could not be relied upon to refer to the line of the Footpath being discussed. It was plainly obvious to anyone of sound mind that the contents of the letter referred to the path in question and stated that it was not public, but an occupational path. Mr. Connaughton indicated to the Inspector, that the Barrister was "clutching at straws". Mr. Millman replied "I will decide if he is clutching at straws".

User evidence forms!

The 38 user forms presented to the Elected Members of Beds. County Council (The decision makers) in 1995 were discussed.

The "Council" based their case presented to the committee in 1995 upon the evidence contained within these user forms. In 2013 the validity of these forms was analysed by two Parish Councilors who were born and resided in Maulden most of their lives. The analysis indicated that none were valid. A further analysis was conducted by Mr. Bowers using information discovered in "The Council" files (Charts, interviews, forms) etc. The more comprehensive analysis revealed that only 5 of the 38 people who submitted User Forms could have used the path for the 20- year period 1936/1956. Of those 5, not one could have been considered as members of the general public.

Therefore, Section 31 of the Highways Act 1980, could not have been satisfied. Beds. County Council, (1995), the Inspector (Mr. Holley 1997), and Central Beds. Council Officers; have always based the dedication of footpath 28 using the evidence contained in the 38 User Forms submitted. Although this was newly submitted evidence, (Since 1997), the Inspector Mr. Millman stated [Quote] "In **my** view the cross- examination revealed that the evidence contained in the chart was essentially the same evidence as that considered by the Inspector in 1997. It cannot be considered new evidence. The Analysis also contained no new relevant evidence". **The Inspector had previously stated that he would consider the Analysis of the User Evidence Forms as relevant and new evidence**

Mr. Millman (the Inspector and former Rights of Way

Officer) did not appear to, or had no intention of accepting, the fundamental issue; [The evidence placed before him proved that Section 31 of the Highways Act had not been satisfied. Therefore the path had not been dedicated as a Public Right of Way,] The evidence contained in the chart and User forms considered by Mr. Holley (Inspector) in 1997 had not been analysed or tested, he was therefore misdirected by Beds. County Council when they based their whole case upon the User Evidence Forms.

Note! In paragraph 24 of the Inspectors decision letter, Mr. Millman states "Mr Bowers appeared to concede at the Inquiry that this argument showed a misunderstanding of the law".

Note! Mr. Bowers is not qualified to interpret or question the Law.

Mr. Millman (Inspector) did not, or would not consider the fact that the evidence contained in the 38 User Forms did not satisfy Section 31 Highways Act 1980.

Note! From the very start of this case in 1995 when the Council added Footpath 28 to the Modified Map, the only evidence they relied upon were the User Evidence Forms.

The Authors of the report presented to the Committee 19th. July 1995, (Glen Kilday, Directorate of Leisure Services) and (John Atkinson, Head of Legal & Member Services) informed the members. [Quote] "Most of the Documentary evidence which has been discovered is of no assistance in ascertaining if the path is a public Right of Way or not".

Note! No reference to County Surveyors letter dated 21st. October 1957 stating that the [path was an Occupational Path which of course is not a Public path]. The Authors of the report therefore relied upon the 38 submitted User Forms, and concluded that [Quote], "The officers are of the view that it is a reasonable conclusion that on balance the path is more likely to be a public right of way than not". The Councilor for the area Councilor Sollars, informed the Council that he did not consider the evidence submitted proved that the track had footpath status.

Mr. Millman (Inspector) did not consider this information, but relied upon the opinion of Mr. Holley (Inspector) in 1997.

SUMMARY;

It has been shown that Mr Millman (Inspector) was not prepared to have **ALL** available evidence revealed to the Public attending the Public Inquiry, but was content to listen to, and allow statements and comments to be presented by objectors to the appeal eg. Barrister, Council Officers, Open Spaces Society, East Herts Footpath Society.
The closing statements by Mr. Connaughton and Mrs. Marlene Masters, using evidence and legal cases, revealed the unjust and unnecessary aspects of this Public Inquiry.

Mr. Millman's, refusing to allow Mr. Bowers to read his opening and witness statements to the Public; [thereby preventing the public from knowing of the Councils disingenuous and culpable actions], is an indication of the determination of certain parties to ensure that the truth was not revealed. Mr. Bowers was also prevented from questioning the Council officials, which again would have revealed the measures taken by the "Council" to obstruct the wishes of the elected members (The decision makers).

In a letter dated 26th. February 2015 from Mr. Carr (CEO) Central Bedfordshire Council, Mr. Bowers was declared **VEXATIOUS** because he continued to asked certain questions, which the council were not prepared to answer. This was an attempt to silence Mr. Bowers, and they ("The Council") will therefore not accept or respond to any communications concerning this distressing and unnecessary situation.

It can be assumed that this Schedule 14 appeal was orchestrated to ensure that no condemnation or wrongdoing could be attributed to any Authority or organisation, which could result in compensation being paid or legal proceeding being taken. It appears the Inspector made up the rules and law as he went along.

All quotes used in this document can be substantiated by statements made during the Inquiry, which are available on the Filming and Recordings of the Inquiry proceedings!

Note! A [Letter before Action] will be submitted with a request for Judicial Review Submitted by: Mr. A. Bowers 123B Clophill Rd. Maulden, Beds. MK45 2AE
Tel. 01525 860036, E.mail: bowers-alan@sky.com

CHAPTER: IV
APPRAISAL OF DECISION

Appraisal of decision letter dated 2nd. October 2015 by Government Inspector Peter Millman
APPEAL REF: FPS/P0420/14A/1R
APPRAISAL OF DECISSION MADE BY INSPECTOR PETER MILLMAN OF A PUBLIC INQUIRY HELD 15th. 16th September 2015 TO APPEAL AGAINST THE DECISION OF CENTRAL BEDFORDSHIRE COUNCIL NOT TO MAKE AN ORDER TO DELETE FOOTPATH 28 MAULDEN.

1/. The reason for the Public Inquiry was because a previous decision by Inspector Mark Yates in September 2013. had been Quashed. Note! The Inquiry (September 2015) has taken 2 years to convene because of delays concerning the Inspectorate. The date of the Inquiry had been changed several times.

Preliminary Matters:

1. The statement. "This type of appeal is usually dealt with by means of written representation" is because that is the method usually advised by the Inspectorate. The proceedings were videoed and recorded at my request and paid for by myself.

2. His last sentence states he would alert me. He did not allow me to present my opening statement or my witness statement because. "it would take up too much time and, He did not consider the contents of the statements were relevant to the case'' (his words), he stated that he would accept it as read, because the council were in possession

of a copy. I understood that it was a public Inquiry, and the public should be made aware of all evidence concerning the case. Most of the evidence within my statements revealed the reason why the Inquiry was taking place.

Because I was not allowed to reveal the contents of my statement (evidence); it allowed the actions and conduct of council officers to go unchallenged.

Background:

Para. 4/ Inspector states. "in 2008 Mr. Bowers made an application for an order to delete the path from the Definitive Map, following unsuccessful attempts to extinguish it under the Highways Act 1980." He did not inform the Public that the application was made on the advice of the Beds. County Council. 21st. August 2008. Also, that Central Beds, issued an order to Extinguish the path using Section 118 Highways Act. on 13th. May 2013. They also issued an order to Stop Up the path using Section 116 Highways Act. on 13th. June 2013. These orders were issued at the request of the elected members at the meeting held 13th. February 2013. Note! This inquiry is concerning the decisions made at the meeting held 13th. February 2013. The Inspector denied me the opportunity of informing the Public of all these events; because he prevented me giving my opening statement, and witness statement. Because (In his words) "it would take up too long and he did not consider the contents of the statement were Relevant to the case"

Whether any new evidence has been produced:

Para 14/ The Inspector states "It seems to me that 'new evidence' can only be evidence, which was not before the ultimate decision maker, the Inspector". The decision makers (in the first instance) were the Sub Committee which met in 1995. The Inspector in 1997 was not provided with a true analysis of the user evidence presented to the sub- committee, (only, the chart Appendix 7 of the council's bundle)

Para.15/ The Inspector states: 'The council produced, at the 2015 Inquiry, a table said to have been produced before the 1997 Inquiry and Possibly before the Committee Meeting in 1995. (No dates or proof). Why would it differ from the chart supplied to the Committee (Appendix 7)? The Inspector also states that "In My view it is likely that Inspector Holley took his figure of 13 from this table". He is referring to the table which could possibly have been produced at the Committee Meeting. (Not very convincing).

Para. 17/ The Inspector states; "In my view the cross examination revealed that the evidence contained in the chart (My analysis) was essentially the same as that considered by the Inspector in 1997. It cannot be considered new evidence." There is considerably more evidence contained in my analysis (from evidence revealed in Council's bundle). There could only have been 5 people who supplied User Evidence Forms that were able to have used the disputed path during the period 1936-1956. Of those 5 none could be considered members of the public. The Inspector appears to ignore This Fact.

Para 22/ The Inspector when considering Section 31 Highways Act 1980; states.
    "Mr. Bowers appeared to concede at the Inquiry that this argument showed a misunderstanding of the law". I am not qualified to question the Law. But I understand that the 20-year period referred to in Section 31 Highways Act 1980 means 20 years not less.

Para 24/ The Inspectors appears to disregard any evidence given at the Inquiry stating that use of the path was permissive. (Sworn statement by Mr. Sharp Co- owner of the land between 1946- 1956).

Para. 25/ The period in question was 1936-1956 the council's chart clearly shows that only 5 of the users could have used the path during that time, and none of those 5 could be considered members of the public at large.

Para.26/ Referring to the last line in Para.26 There is sufficient reason (User Evidence) that the evidence considered by Inspector Holly in 1997 should be re- evaluated.

Para 28/ Again the Inspector is expressing his view that the law is being misunderstood regarding the status of an Occupational Way. An Occupational path can only be considered public if it has dual status. It was confirmed by the County Surveyor in 1957 that the path only had Occupational status.

Para 29/ The Inspector is again questioning the Qualification and actions of the County Surveyor in 1997, because it seems to him it was a presumption of regularity. He also states that it is assumed the action of the Surveyor was lawful, but states that he may not have had knowledge of all relevant facts to arrive at a correct conclusion Is there any evidence to indicate that the Surveyor my not have been competent enough to assess the situation asked of him?

Para 30/ The Inspector also rejects the argument put forward by Mrs. Masters with respect to the person or persons who compiled the Definitive Map for Bedfordshire would have carried out their tasks correctly....Again, is there any evidence to doubt the ability of the person/persons who compiled the Definitive Map.

Para 31/ Again, the Inspector is questioning the conveyancing of the property when sold in 1946. He states. "That is, in my view an assertion without evidential foundation".

Para 32/ In answer to Mr. Connaughton's statement referring to. "people of sound mind" The Inspectors states. "That is not an argument based, as far as this route is concerned, on evidence." No! It is based on common sense!

Para 33/ The Inspector appears to be content to reject any comment made by the Inspector Mark Yates in his decision which was Quashed. Mr. Yates agreed that the appeal route was not a "designated right of way prior to 1997". Mr. Millman states. "It is clear to me that the Inspector's statement indicated nothing more than that the appeal route was not included in the Definitive Map and Statement prior to 1997."

Para 34/ The Inspector is again questioning the Evidence of Mr. Connaughton and Mrs. Masters that the owners of the land crossed by the Path, 1936-1956 could not and would not have dedicated public rights of way across it. Mr. Millman states "It seems to me that these arguments miss the fundamental point that to satisfy the test in S31 of the Highways Act 1980. the fundamental point that to satisfy the test in S31 of the Highways Act 1980 (paragraph 11 above) actual dedication does not need to be proved. Upon the satisfaction of the test, dedication is Deemed to have occurred, in other words, the effect of qualifying use of the route is the same as 'if dedication had actually occurred". Mr. Millman does not seem understand the Fundamental Point, that the test has not been satisfied.

Proceedings which occurred during Inquiry as shown on Video.

The purpose and indeed the tile of Inquiry indicates that it is a schedule 14 appeal against the decision made by Central Bedfordshire Council not to approve an application under Section 53 of the Wildlife and Countryside Act to Delete Footpath 28 from the Definitive Map.

In his opening statement, Mr. Millman stated "I have given a great deal of thought to the way the evidence should be presented, the statement of evidence as originally sent to the Inspectorate were too long, {if we were bound by the Inquiry rules], then anyone who had a statement of more than 1500 words would have had to provide a summary which would be read out at the Inquiry. Now! Mr. Maciejewski has now provided a summary of his rather long proof of evidence, now! I am not aware that you (Mr. Bowers) has provided the same" Mr. Bowers informed the Inspector that he had contacted the Inspectorate and informed Ms. Baylis that he could not condense his statement into 1500 words. He was told that he could present his statement at the Inquiry.

After refusing to allow Mr. Bowers to read his Witness Statement and Opening statement. He informed the Inquiry that "anything that happened after 1997 are irrelevant and I am not prepared to waste the time of this Inquiry to listen to material that cannot be relevant to my decision."

"This inquiry is not about what has happened since 1997. not about that"

He also stated "Mr. Bowers has printed his statement but not circulated it; so in the circumstances, Mr. Bowers has printed it but not circulated it yet. So, I am going to accept it as read so that the Council can then concentrate on the relevant material in cross-examination, I am not going to have that 29-

page statement which cannot be my concern by law read out." A member of the public said to the Inspector "With respect, this is a non-statutory Inquiry it is not governed, as you said in your opening by 2007 rules, so anything goes."

Mr Millman replied "That is not the case". After a response from the member of public, Mr. Millman in a frustrated manner said." I have said and I am not going to say it anymore, that the bulk of the 29 page statement does not contain evidence which I am allowed to take into consideration, so, I am not going to hear it, we can accept it as read because the Council have seen it, everyone else will have a look at it, so we do not have to waste the time of this Inquiry on irrelevant material, that is irrelevant to the point of the Inquiry, that is to decide Mr. Bowers Appeal. At one stage Mr. Bowers asked the inspector if he was concerned about the actions of Council officers.

Mr. Millman States "I am not allowed by law to consider the actions of officers". He goes onto say "Anything that happened subsequent to 1997 is not my concern " but agreed that information concerning actions of officers should be subject to criminal proceedings or Judicial Review.

Other Matters:

Para 37/ Mr. Millman made it clear that he would not hear/ allow my Opening Statement and Witness Statement but accepted them as read because the Council had a copy of them. The Members of the Public attending the Public Meeting were therefore not made aware of the actions and conduct of certain Public Officers, which was the original reason this Inquiry was requested.

CONCLUSION:

The Inspector, Mr. Millman directed by The Secretary of State DEFRA to preside over this Non- Statutory Public Inquiry appears to have disregarded any evidence produced to allow this appeal but has accepted the Fragile case presented by the Council to reject it.

It can also be shown (on film), the Inspector showed no interest in the closing statements of Mr. Connaughton, and Mrs. Masters. He looked at documents occasionally, but most of the time showed no interest and is seen looking around the room and making no notes. While the members of the public, are seen to be listening intensely. The Barrister declined the opportunity of cross-examining Mr. Connaughton or Mrs. Masters.

Alan Bowers
Ein-Ty, 123b Clophill Rd. Maulden, Beds. MK45 2AE
Dated. 8th. October2015

CHAPTER: V

Part 9. Banister continues to talk about irrelevant material. He Appears frustrated at responses from Alan. Inspector states misunderstanding.

Part 10. Barrister continues with cross examination, referring to irrelevant material

Part 11. Barrister tries to discredit analysis of User Evidence Forms. Appears frustrated. Continued next day.

Day 2. 16th. September:

Part 1. Inspector tries to explain his reason for introducing Mrs. Wiseman's document.

Richard questions Mr. Maciejewski (Mr. Mac) concerning report presented to committee 13th. Feb 2013, Mr. Mac appears uneasy. Inspector intervenes to reduce burden on Mr. Mac Inspector again states "This is a matter for the court".

Part 2. Mr. Bowers wants to question Mr. Mac. Inspector appears irritated and refuses to allow questions to be put to Mr. Mac.

Mrs. Masters questions Mr. Mac who again appears uneasy. He appears to look at Inspector for guidance. Inspector intervenes many times to reduce burden upon Mi⁻. Mac

Part 3. Mrs. Masters continues to question Mr. Mac. who continues to be uneasy.

Part 4. Mrs. Masters continues to question Mr. MacBarrister asks Mr. Mac. questions.

Part 5. Barrister continues to ask Mr. Mac questions. Mrs. Masters again objects to late admission of Barrister.

Part 6. Mr. Westley, Mrs. Rumfit, and Barrister make statements.

Part 7. Continued statement by Barrister.

Part 8. Continued statement by Barrister.

Part 9. Continued statement by Barrister.

Part 10. Short film after lunch.

Part 11. Closing statement by Richard...beginning of closing statement by Mrs. Masters.

Part 12. Closing statement by Mrs. Masters.

Part 13. Closing statement by Mrs. Masters

Part 14. Closing statement by Mrs. Masters.

Part 15. Continued closing statement by Mrs. Masters... Barrister declines to cross examine Mrs. Masters... Inspector closes Inquiry.

CHAPTER: VI

PROTOCOL LETTER to APPLY FOR JUDICIAL REVIEW:

Mr Alan Bowers, Ein-Ty, 123B Clophill Road, Maulden, Bedfordshire, MK45 2AE Tel: 01525 860036 Email: bowers-alan@sky.com

PRE-ACTION PROTOCOL BRIEF
referring to
The Appeal Decision by Peter Millman BA Reference
FPS/PO420/14A/1R dated 2 October 2015

1. Judicial Review affords members of the public an opportunity to ask a Judge of the lawfulness of a Decision passed down by a Government Department. I submit five Grounds, reasons why I believe Mr Millman erred in law in coming to his Decision to refuse my Appeal. The First Ground, <u>Procedural Irregularities</u> is fundamental. These quasi-judicial arrangements can be seen to be not as the law intended. The loopholes are being exploited by interested parties to corrupt the due process. The Second Ground; <u>The Inspector failed to give any proper weight to Relevant Evidence</u> is identical to two earlier cases in which DEFRA conceded due to their appointed Inspectors' failure to consider all relevant evidence in coming to their Decisions. The other three grounds examined with narratives as precursors to the Statement of Facts relied upon are:

- Ground Three. The Decision.
- Ground Four: Bad Law, Bad Officials
- Ground Five: Ineligibility.

Context

2.   The Fraternity is the collective noun used to describe access industry activists in Government employment within DEFRA, the Planning Inspectorates and many of the access departments within Strategic Authorities. They operate either top-down or bottom-up, buttressed by User organisations. They start with the proposition that, because their job is to protect access, they should be suspicious of, and proactive against all those who wish in any way to oppose or alter a right of way. The Inspector straddles DEFRA and the Planning Inspectorate which steers him. Those of the Fraternity mindset are proactive, not averse to taking action to deprive property owners of their possessions. "Behind virtually every recorded instance of obstruction, misrepresentation, bullying and intimidation, there is a government employee."[1] They have control at every level of public contact where they have an in-situ opponent capable of obstructing the aspirations for justice of home or property owners. Mine is such a case. I am representative of many.

Ground 1. Procedural Irregularities

3.   The Inspector would have been aware that he was fulfilling a Function for which he was not qualified. The Planning Inspectorate's Rights of Way Section set out in its Advice Note 19 guidance to Inspectors how they should manage the Human Rights Act 1998. Schedule 1 of that Act sets out particular rights which have been incorporated into UK law from the European Convention on Human Rights as adopted by Parliament in 2000.

---

[1] The Hobhouse Report 2011, p.29, para 14.

4.   Article 6, The Right to a Fair Trial, "concerned with the fairness of the procedure for access to and handling of Inquiries and other procedures for considering objections to orders". At para 10. the Inspectorate claims "an Inspector is independent and impartial for the purposes of Article 6(1)" and quotes as the authority, from Bryan v. UK [1995] 21 EHRR 342.

In 1995, there was a Lord Chancellor's Independent Panel of Inspectors in place, superseded in its entirety in 2001 by a cadre of new Inspectors. Nine of the 11 engaged on casework were drawn from the ranks of former Rights of Way Officers from the Counties.

5.   In para 9, the Advice Note sets out the framework of Article 6(1). "In the determination of his civil rights and obligations .... everyone is entitled to a fair and public hearing within a reasonable time by an independent and impartial tribunal established by law..." The present Inspectors cannot be independent. The policy-maker cannot be the Decision-taker, nor can the Secretary of State be judge and jury in her own 'Court'. The folly in attempting to insist *all* Inspectors are independent and impartial can be immediately dispelled by reference to Inspector Millman's partial behaviour against me. Not only did he prevent me, the appellant, from being heard, but he also produced a Decision carefully assembled with selected elements of evidence. The delivery of his Decision revealed not the mandatory independent, impartial Inspector but an unreformed, unscrupulously dismissive opponent.

6.   By definition, the Lower Court or Tribunal should be chaired by a qualified barrister or solicitor. That is the law. A quasi-judicial public inquiry is not structured as a Court. It is illegal. Neither the Secretary of State nor Inspectors have the authority to judge land issues. Evidence is not given on oath.

The Hobhouse Report 2011, p.29, para 14. The Act specifies Tribunals not Inquiries.[2]

1. Para 23 ii of Advice Note 19 identifies equality of arms as possibly falling within the Inspector's remit: "each party must have a reasonable chance to put their case and must not be placed at a substantial disadvantage to another party".

• Malpractice had led to the failure of the first attempt by the Fraternity' to defeat me. DEFRA conceded. The errant Inspector was replaced by Mr Millman. DEFRA took the opportunity during the pause to reinforce the opposition, allowing representation, in addition to the new Inspector and local authority, by professional people representing the Ramblers and Open Spaces Society. There is nothing in the language of Schedule 14(4)(1) which provides for the belated entry of interested third parties into these proceedings. Parliament did not provide an opening for the production of evidence against the Appellant *during* the Appeal procedure.

• Inspector Millman chose to be the custodian of my Statement of Case document. Nothing comes to mind of my case material being aired either during the course of the Inquiry or within an opinionated Decision document.

• I had exhausted my life's savings in the attempt to defend my property. The opposition use the cost of justice as a deterrent. I could not afford qualified legal representation at the Inquiry. There was me and two others, a trio of OAPs defending my rights, one of whom, engaged to counterbalance Counsel, joined the trio at the last moment. I was distressed to discover (I was not informed) that the Local Authority had engaged at public expense a specialist London barrister supported by a solicitor to ensure I did not succeed. It was procedurally unacceptable to fail to notify me, particularly

---

[2] The Act specifies Tribunals not Inquiries.

given my inexperience as to the procedure that Counsel had been instructed at the eleventh hour. It was in their interest to see I did not succeed. The failure to allow me sight of Counsel's case was to my disadvantage. The Inspector said he was aware or "the inequality of arms" issue yet chose to exacerbate the situation.

Ground 2. The Inspector failed to give any proper weight to Relevant Evidence

8.   On 4 October 2013, the High Court Judge, Mr Justice Holgate QC, considered an application for Judicial Review in respect of the Peppard siblings. He found the Government Inspector, Ms Doran MIPROW, had erred in law through her failure to consider all relevant evidence. He approved Judicial Review, saying *in obiter,* the matter required 'ventilation'. DEFRA, not wanting ventilation, conceded.

9.   As a consequence of manipulation and wrongdoing at Central Bedfordshire Council's (CBC's) Development Management Committee (DMC), I was steered into appealing CBC's refusal to delete the wrongfully designated FP28. I suspected an ambush. I was right. The Inspectorate:

• Suppressed my dossier of evidence, intentionally named 'Ventilation - The Bowers Case' so that the connection with Mr Justice Holgate's reminder of relevance of evidence should not be lost. The dossier contained two important strands of new evidence:

o   A certificate by two senior Parish Councillors from Maulden, a Parish which has never laid claim to FP28, certifying that, of the 38 friends and relatives to have submitted User Cards, not one was valid. The public does not lightly assert against its rights.

o   Documentary evidence, proof that the County Council's Officials had been active in the recruiting of my opponents.

•   The Inspector ignored the first of my cases, the first Ground of which was identical to that on which Mr Justice Holgate had already ruled. It formed no part in contributing to his Decision.

I appealed. DEFRA conceded. Mr Millman was appointed to take the case forward.

10.   My Witness Statement was lodged with the Inspectorate in June 2015, followed nearer the date of Inquiry by my Opening Statement. At home, I read through the Witness Statement which I timed at 1 hour and 20 minutes. I was the appellant. My Opening Statement took 10 minutes to read.

11.   My Witness Statement had been with the Inspectorate for three months. It did not attract comment. Since it had been the CBC's rejection of my Section 53 application, my evidence included the malpractice experienced on 13 February 2013 at the DMC. Unexpectedly, on the first day of the Inquiry[3] the Inspector, Mr Millman, said he would only hear evidence up to the Decision made by Inspector Holley in 1997. That was the first I heard of that limitation. I was reluctantly reconciled to losing the latter part of my evidence.

That left a substantial element of relevant fact remaining up to and including 1997 and the consequences arising therefrom.

12.   I protested the Inspector's decision and timing. He is shown on film as saying: "Iam not prepared to waste the time of the Inquiry because it is too long and *most* of the contents are not relevant to the case". The duration of the Inquiry was planned for three days but it was concluded in under two days.

---

[3] As shown in the document 'Enough', p.6, para 12.

His decision generated protests from both sides of the fence. In her Statement, Mrs Marlene Masters, a supporter, told the Inspector it was possible to separate the wheat from whatever he believed to be chaff. Mr Westley of the East Herts Footpath Society suggested the appellant be allowed to read his Statement so that the relevant points arising could be considered.

13.　The Inspector remained resolute in refusing me the right for my relevant evidence to be heard, the third such Inspector to have done so in this cycle. He did not give full and appropriate weight to what I had to say, giving instead disproportionate weight to the irrelevant evidence of others. It is intolerable that members of the public identified as owning desirable property coveted by unaccountable members of politically and doctrinally motivated officials of the public service should be targeted in this way. A second dossier with the secondary title 'Ventilation', to make the point with Inspectors, and entitled 'The Bowers Case II' was subjected to the same maltreatment as the earlier Bowers Case dossier.

Ground 3. The Decision

14.　I want to expose the Decision's bias through examples of untruthfulness and scheming:
　• At para 24 of his Decision, the Inspector wrote, "no new evidence was produced to the 2015 Inquiry which suggested that permission was granted by a landowner between 1936-1956 to any person to use the path or that any private rights were granted or claimed". That was untrue and would have been known to have been untrue. During the Inquiry there was a lengthy discussion of this new evidence involving the Inspector, the Authority's Mr Maciejewski and Mrs Masters. Mr Sharp the owner had made a statutory declaration^ as to fact. The film reveals Mrs.Masters saying to Mr Maciejewski,

"do you agree Mr Sharp gave permission?" He agreed that in his Statutory Declaration the former land owner Mr. Sharp, had "given permission" to the users of his private land (which defeats a claim of user "as of right") Mr Sharp had therefore not dedicated his path to the public as claimed. Appendix C to CBC's submission to the Inspectorate for the Inspector's use reveals: "During the early 1950s Mr Sharp permitted a few people whom he knew to use the track as a short cut". Mr Sharp's statutory declaration, on oath, defeats any attempt to argue presumed dedication, a fact of which Mr Millman would be aware. The Inspector had no regard to the locality through which the alleged path goes. The Inspector found as fact something on which there was nothing to rely upon, that is, he gave weight to irrelevant evidence, deciding that evidence of use, was as "of right", that is without permission and that Mr. Sharp had intended to dedicate his land to the use of the general public

• Mr Millman's circulation of an irrelevant document regarding a dissimilar case involving a Mrs Debbie Wiseman unsubtly revealed the difference between what happened at a quasi-judicial Inquiry and what would not happen in a Court of Law. In Court, a Judge does not openly solicit for a side he supports. I did not, could not, understand why Mr Millman was keen to distribute documents relating to a case with no bearing on my case. I am aware Mrs Wiseman complained to no avail to the Inspectorate's in-house complaints agency, Quality Assurance. Mr Millman should now[r] be asked to account for his irrational behaviour. These quasi-judicial hearings are of themselves *ultra vires* because DEFRA has no powers to make any decisions on private land when the land in question has never been a highway and never been legitimately public at any time previously.

Ground 4. Bad Law, Bad Officials

15.   Parts of Section 31(1) of the Highways Act 1980 have been identified as bad law. It depends for most of its success upon Government Officials supported by User Groups. Section 31 provides the opportunity for groups in significant numbers to associate with a view to converting private paths to public status by creating a weight of numbers to suffocate what would normally be one or two property owners. Known since 2011 as the Cheats' Charter,[4] the goal is achieved by way of fraudulent claims of 20 years uninterrupted use of a path or way. In 1997, Inspector Holley announced the relevant period to be 1936-1956.

Vernon Lowe of Cumbria said: "Everyone has given up fighting the Ramblers and particularly the horse riders in this part of Cumbria because the Inspectors in all the Inquiries have always sided with the applicants on the grounds that they must be right rather than the objectors because they outnumber them by 20:1. The facts are irrelevant".

16.   In 1995 Bedford CC's Rights of Way Sub Committee had been told of the then 35 Individual User Cards submitted by claimants, compared with three landowners. Officials put that information in front of Inspector Holley who conducted a written representation procedure Inquiry of the evidence he had been given. The Inspector took at face value the multiplicity of fraudulent claims put before him. Inspector Millman was presented with documentary evidence[5] revealing County Officials to have been involved in the creation of the body of opposition against me. He made no comment.

---

[4] The Hobhouse Report 2011

[5] 'Ventilation - The Bowers Case II', p.27. Inspector Millman blocked all relevant evidence in that document in precisely the same way 'Ventilation - The Bowers Case' had been suppressed.

17.   Senior Authority Solicitor Atkinson, who led the assault on my property, refused to answer questions arising from the move towards the wrongful creation of the public footpath through my home in 1995. It should be assumed that proper procedures were followed in putting the path on the Definitive Map, that proper evidence existed but only "in the absence of evidence to the contrary".[6] CBC's CEO claimed the /<w prevented the Authority from giving me a fair and impartial hearing. He has resisted all requests to divulge on which part of the law he depended for perverting the course of justice. The Authority had formally declared me to be 'vexatious' so as to avoid answering difficult questions. On 7 August 2013, the two senior Councillors of Maulden Parish Council examined what had now become 38 User Evidence Cards confined to a study of friends and relatives. Their conclusion: "none of the user forms presented to Committee" in 1995 "were valid". I conducted a separate time and space examination of the bar chart used by the Officials in their deliberations. I observed only five claimants could have had uninterrupted use of the path 1936-1956. Dorset County Council has ruled that five is an insufficient number to justify change.[7] Each of our five was found to be self-disqualifying.

18.   Section 31(1) is a many-faceted Section.

• The first limb of Section 31(1) provides the test which has to be met by the claimant - "evidence of unchallenged, uninterrupted use for 20 years". This is difficult to achieve. In 1957, the year after the last of those 20 years, the County Surveyor told the claimant, Mrs Izzard, in a letter dated 21 October 1957, the path in question was a private, occupation

---

[6] Trevelyan v. Secretary of State for Environment, Transport and Regions [2001] EWCA CN 244.

[7] R v. SSETR (exp. Dorset [1999] and R v. SSETR *ex parte* Dorset CC [1999] NPC. 72.

path. Inspector Holley agreed. Mrs Izzard took no further action for 36 years, after which a consortium of Bedfordshire County Council Rights of Way Officials, Ms Ashbrook of the Open Spaces Society and Mr Clarke of Bedfordshire Rights of Way Association became increasingly militant in targeting me.

• The second limb is a proviso: *"unless...*there is sufficient evidence to demonstrate that the landowner had no intention to dedicate..."* Reference to Ground 3, The Decision, reveals at para 14 the certitude that Mr Sharp had no intention of opening up his market garden for the free passage of people who were the buyers of his produce. Mr Millman pays no heed to the effect the adjoining path had when he avoided a rational conclusion. Nor is Councillor Lockey's evidence given consideration in pointing out the traditional route to Maulden Woods, a converging path only 60 yards away at its most distant, which conveniently takes the general public to where they want to go.

• There is more to read from Section 31(1) indicative of the Inspector having come to a decision on the evidence that no other person is likely to have reached given proper legal weight to the situation. "Where a way over any land other than a way of such *character* that use of it by the public could not give rise at common law" to any presumption of dedication. Mrs Masters and PINS (it featuring in their consistency guidelines) drew the attention of Inspector Millman to the Thornhill v. Weeks [1914] decision as one of the legal references available to him, indicating he must consider the character of the way. In 1914 the no-go factor was a stable yard. In this case it was a market garden in which produce - cabbages, lettuce, strawberries etc - grew; not the place to which the marauding public would be offered unlimited transit. *They did not need to.* The Inspector failed to give any proper weight to relevant evidence and gave disproportionate weight to irrelevant evidence.

43

19. Nowhere in Section 31 does it say *who* will test evidence. That is found in Section 32 which buttresses not only Section 31 and Article 6 of the Human Rights Act 1998, but also my First Ground - Procedural Irregularities It says, "a Court or Tribunal", There is no mention of illegal, problematical, quasi-judicial arrangements.

Ground 5. Ineligibility

20. On 15 September 2015, at the Inquiry, Mr Connaughton said in his Opening Statement: "Mrs Izzard, the claimant, was a member of the family who owned the property between 1936-1946, half the 20 years claimed. It is trite law that a landowner cannot claim the exercise of a public right of way when formerly, use was by way of private right. Mrs Izzard and her family and relatives could not have claimed a public right of way on their own land by virtue of their own family's private use".

21. Two separate analyses of the 38 User Evidence Cards revealed not one to be valid. Referring to the Parish's submission, the Authority's Mr Maciejewski acknowledge that, of the 38: "It is interesting that every person is in some way connected to the Izzards".[8]

• This means Inspector Holley in 1997, working under written representation procedures,[9] tested none of the evidence, evidence which to some degree was created fraudulently.[10] The Inspector took at face value the entirety of

---

[8] Email to Sutton, 17 September 2013.

[9] "I was not advised by officials I would forfeit my right to cross-examine witnesses and their evidence"- Alan Bowers.

[10] The Inspector admits in his Decision Letter FPS/M0200/7/25 dated 26 August 1997, he had heard of the discrepancies. He asked the Council to identify them! The answer satisfied him that the discrepancies "are not of such gravity as to invalidate the evidence" (45)." No further test can be applied to the evidence without recourse to an Inquiry (46)", said Inspector Holley, the appointed Chairman of the Inquiry.

fraudulent, ineligible User Cards put before him. He was not informed of Mr. Sharp's statutory Declaration in which he expressed his intention to limit the use of the route through his property (42). It is recognised in law that a landowner would be unlikely to be churlish and prevent his friends and neighbours the privilege of a short walk through his property to their homes. Declaration on oath is inconvertible as to the landowner's intention.

- The Opening Statement at the Inquiry concluded: "...there is no case with which to proceed. The taking of Maulden FP28 was a wrongful designation".

Signed........Alan Bowers..................................

Dated. 30th. November 2015

CHAPTER: VII
Response to Protocol Letter to Government Legal Department dated 30/11/2015

Government
Legal Department

	Litigation Group T 020 7210 3000
Mr A Bowers	One Kemble Street
Ein-Ty	London
123B Clophill Road	WC2B 4TS
Maulden	
Bedfordshire	
MH45 2AE	DX 123242 Kingsway 6 www.gov.uk/gld

Also by Email

Your ref: -
Our ref: Z1530338/PNK/B5

22 December 2015

Dear Mr Bowers

Alan Bowers v Secretary of State for Environment, Food and Rural Affairs
Proposed Claim for Judicial Review

We write in response to your letter before claim dated 30 November 2015, and are instructed by the proposed Defendant in this matter, namely the Secretary of State for Environment, Food and Rural Affairs ("the Secretary of State"). Please note that the Planning Inspectorate should not be named as a proposed defendant in the proposed claim as the Inspector is appointed by and on behalf of the Secretary of State.

For the reasons set out below, we consider that your proposed claim is without merit, and we invite you to reconsider your stated intention to pursue the claim. In the event that a claim for judicial review is pursued, it will be resisted, and if successful the Secretary of State will seek her costs of doing so.

1 - The Claimant

The proposed Claimant is Alan Bowers.

2 - The Defendant

The proposed Defendant is the Secretary of State for Environment, Food and Rural Affairs.

3 ■ Reference Details

All correspondence should quote reference Z1530338/PNK/B5. The principal lawyer dealing with this claim is Prachi Kanse.

4 • Details of the Matter being challenged

The proposed challenge is to the decision of an Inspector, appointed on behalf of the Secretary of State, to hear an appeal under paragraph 4 of Schedule 14 to the Wildlife and Countryside Act 1981 ("the 1981 Act"). That appeal was made against the decision of Central Bedfordshire Council ("the Council") not to make an

Lee John-Charles - Head of Division
Neera Gajjar - Deputy Director, Team Leader Litigation B5

Le\cel
ProcUce Quality
LawSociety -

order under section 53(2) of the 1981 Act, pursuant to an application by you to delete the footpath from the Council's Definitive Map and Statement.

The "issue" is whether the Appeal Decision is flawed on any of the grounds set out in your letter before action.

5 - Response to Proposed Claim

1. Your proposed grounds of challenge are addressed in turn below.

2. We make some general observations here first about the role of the court in a claim for judicial review:

    (i) The court is not concerned with the *merits* of the decision, in the sense of re-deciding questions of fact or judgment. All matters relating to the weighing of evidence are for the Inspector, not the court: see for example *R (Newsmith) v SSEFRA* [2001] EWHC (Admin) 74.

    (ii) The only exception to this will be where a factual finding is perverse but proving perversity in public law is an exceptionally high hurdle. It requires that the decision maker has taken leave of his senses (see again *Newsmith*).

    (iii) The court can only intervene where it can be shown that the Inspector has erred in law, including my making a factual finding that is perverse: *E and R v SSHD* [2004] 1 QB 1044.

    (iv) An Inspector considering an appeal under paragraph 4 of Schedule 14 to the 1981 Act has a defined jurisdiction, to consider whether the relevant highway authority had been wrong to refuse to make an order under section 53 of the 1981 Act. In this case that in turn engages the question posed in section 53(3)(c)(iii), as to whether evidence had been discovered which, when taken with other available evidence, showed that there was no public right of way over land shown in the Definitive Map and Statement as a highway. For the reasons given by the Inspector at paragraphs 6-9 of his decision, therefore, the critical question for him was as summarised in paragraph 9:

    > 9. *The principal issues therefore are whether any new evidence has been produced and, if so, whether, when considered with all other relevant evidence, it shows on the balance of probabilities that there is no public right of way over footpath 28 ...*

    (v) It also follows from this that the Inspector's task was not to conduct a wide-ranging inquiry into the propriety of the conduct of your application to delete Footpath 28 by the Council and others. Rather, he was right to focus on the cogency of the evidence relating to use of the path by the public in the period 1936 to 1956.

Grounds 1: Procedural irregularities

3. Your letter sets out a series of assertions, both as to fact and law, for which you do not provide any evidence or authority, and which are wholly without foundation:

    (I) The Inspector was fully qualified to perform the function that he was performing, of an Inspector appointed by the Secretary of State to hear an appeal under paragraph 4 of Schedule 14 to the 1981 Act. You point to no domestic legal authority for the proposition that an Inspector has to be a qualified barrister or solicitor, and there is no such requirement.

    (ii) You quote *Bryan v UK* [1995] 21 EHRR 342, apparently for the proposition that an Inspector, as part of government, cannot be an "independent and impartial" tribunal for the purposes of Article 6 ECHR. So far as that is applicable here, *Bryan* was considered by the House of Lords in *R (Alconbury Developments Ltd) v SSETR* [2003] 2 AC 296, where it was held that the Impartial fact finding role of the Inspector, coupled with judicial review, provided sufficient safeguards to meet the overall requirements of Article 6. The same would be true of the Schedule 14 appeal process, whereby judicial review is available in the same way as in *Alconbury*.

    (iii) You refer the conduct of the Inspector in the present case as illustrating your general point that Inspectors are not impartial. Your individual complaints in this regards are addressed below but, even if correct, they do not demonstrate any structural problem which gives rise to a complaint under Article 6 ECHR precisely because the High Court can, on a claim for judicial review, remedy any unfairness in the process in the individual case.

(iv) The fact that the Secretary of State conceded earlier claims for judicial review by you says nothing about the legality of the decision in this case. It simply shows that judicial review does provide an effective remedy where an Inspector can be shown to have made an error of law.

Ground 2: Inspector failed to give any proper weight to relevant evidence

4. As we have already pointed out, an allegation that a decision maker has given inappropriate "weight" to a piece of evidence, or all evidence seen in the round, does not provide grounds for judicial review. The weighing of the evidence in this case was a matter for the Inspector.

5. In fact, despite the heading, your complaint under this ground does not appear to relate to the weighing of evidence at all. Rather, the main complaint seems to be that the Inspector "suppressed" evidence, namely what you call the "Ventilation Dossier".

6. This is simply incorrect. It is right to say that, In the exercise of his legitimate case management functions, the Inspector did not permit you to present this document in full at the inquiry. The Ventilation Dossier was 29 pages long. You and other witnesses had been invited, prior to the inquiry, to provide summaries of statements which exceeded 1500 words, and you had declined to do this. The Inspector was perfectly entitled to manage the inquiry by controlling the way in which evidence was presented orally. His opening remarks at the inquiry included the following:

> I'm not aware that Mr Bowers has summarised his 29 page statement. As I've indicated already, this statement also contains a good deal of material that cannot be relevant to my decision. It seems to me that in the circumstances the best way to deal with this is to accept his statement as read, since it has   been provided in advance of the inquiry and will be familiar to interested parties. Cross-examination can then concentrate on the essential matter of new evidence and its cogency. Mr Bowers will be free, of course, to make a supplementary oral statement of relevant material which he hadn't put in his original statement, subject of course to a possible short adjournment so that it could be properly considered.'

7. The fact that the Inspector did not permit this evidence to be read out in full does not show that it was ignored or suppressed. On the contrary, it was taken as read.

8. However, the Inspector was plainly correct to say that the Ventilation Dossier contained a good deal of material that was irrelevant to his decision, because it did not go to the question which he had to answer   about whether the public use of the Footpath between 1936 and 1956 was such as to satisfy the test in   section 31 of the Highways Act 1980 ("the 1980 Act").

9. Accordingly, this ground does not demonstrate any arguable error of law by the Inspector.

Ground 3: "The Decision"

10. The first bullet point of paragraph 14 of your letter misquotes paragraph 24 of the Inspector's decision. He did not say that "no new evidence was produced to the 2015 inquiry ...". He actually said:

> ...no significant evidence was produced to the 2015 inquiry which suggested that permission was granted by a landowner between 1936-1956 to any person to use the part or that private rights were   granted or claimed."

11. The distinction between "new" and "significant" evidence is itself significant to your argument. The statement that there was no "significant" evidence reflected an evaluative judgment by the Inspector about the quality of the evidence presented on this issue. The making of such judgments is precisely the function given to the Inspector. The High Court will not interfere with that judgment unless it is perverse. It was plainly not perverse.

12. The rest of your argument in the first two bullet points amounts to no more than disagreement with the Inspector's factual conclusions and does not disclose any legal error by him.

13. Your third bullet point complains of the circulation of an "irrelevant" document by the Inspector, namely the decision of Hoigate J refusing permission to apply for judicial review of the decision of another Inspector in another appeal under para 4 of Schedule 14 involving Mrs Debbie Wiseman, CO / 3097 / 2015. The

-3-

48

Inspector raised Holgate J's decision with the parties in case that had any relevance to the case before him. On analysis, the Inspector did not consider it of direct relevance to this case and placed no particular reliance upon it in his Appeal Decision. It was however a public document which had come to his attention and it was perfectly proper, indeed highly desirable in the interests of fairness, for him to have raised it with *all parties,* in an open way, and invite their comments upon it. It is not arguable that this demonstrates any improper conduct or bias on his part.

Ground 4: Bad law, bad officials

14. Your argument here, appears to amount to a wide-ranging attack on the law and practice relating to the establishment and recording of public rights of way. These complaints have for the most part nothing to do with the defined task of this Inspector, to consider the evidence relating to the existence of Footpath 28.

15. Section 31 of the 1980 Act is part of UK law, enacted by Parliament. It was binding on the Inspector, and is binding on the High Court in a claim for judicial review. To the extent that you consider it to be "bad law", that is a matter you are entitled to raise through the political process, with a view to persuading Parliament to alter or repeal it. For so long as Parliament has not done so, it remains part of UK law and falls to be applied by the Inspector and the Secretary of State.

16. Your arguments at paragraph 19 again relate to the Inspector's conclusions on the facts, and raise no issue of law.

Ground 5: Ineligibility

17. In his decision from 1997, Inspector Holley rejected an argument that the fact that Mrs. Izzard (the applicant for what became Footpath 28) was related to the person who owned the land prior to 1946 meant that use of the path by her had not been as of right. Inspector Holley found that there was evidence of use by members of the public apart from Mrs Izzard and her family, and that was sufficient to constitute use for the purposes of section 31 of the 1980 Act.

18. Your points at paragraph 20 of your letter appear to be an attempt to reopen this issue. However, that does not give grounds for challenging the current decision, for two reasons. First, at least absent clear evidence that it was wrong, the current Inspector was not required to reopen factual findings or judgments made by Inspector Holley. Second, and in any case, the points you make in paragraph 20 of your letter do not show Inspector Holley to have gone wrong. The question of whether Mrs Izzard or some other family member was using the path by right is irrelevant in circumstances where Inspector Holley had found that *other* members of the public were using it as of right.

19. Your further argument at paragraph 21 is no more than a disagreement with a conclusion reached about the facts, albeit in this case a conclusion reached by Inspector Holley in 1997. It gives rise to no issue of law.

Conclusion

20. For the reasons set out above, the Secretary of State does not consider that there is any basis for you to challenge the decision made by the Inspector dated 2 October 2015 and the Secretary of State will not agree to the course proposed in your letter before action.

21. It is considered that your claim is misconceived and should not be pursued. In the event that you do, the Secretary of State will seek her costs if successful in defending the claim.

6 - Details of any Interested Parties

Not applicable

7 - Address for further correspondence and service of court documents

The address for further correspondence and service of Court documents is:

Litigation Team B5
Government Legal Department
One Kemble Street
London WC2B 4TS

DX: 123242 Kingsway
Email: Prachi.Kanse@governmentleQal.Qov.uk

Please mark all correspondence for the attention of Prachi Kanse.

Yours sincerely,

Prachi Kanse
For the Treasury Solicitor

D+44(0)20 7210 3360
F+44(0)20 7210 3001
E prachi.kanse@governmentlegal.gov.uk

CHAPTER: VIII

ATTEMPTS TO OBTAIN JUDICIAL REVIEW: SUMMARY OF EVENTS REGARDING APPLICATION FOR JUDICIAL REVIEW HISTORY
Treasury Solicitor (TSol). Government Legal Dept GLD)

I wrote a Pre-action Protocol letter to TSol. 30th. November 2015; the following is a summary of events regarding that letter.

1/ 22nd. December 2015; I attended Administrative Office (Royal Courts of Justice) and stood in queue for 4 hours to submit application and have it sealed. I was advised the application was being made too late, and that the time to make application had expired. I explained time to submit application did not expire until 2nd. January 2016. However, I was told I must complete Section 8 of form (requesting more time) before my application could be considered.

After application had been sealed, I attended Treasury Solicitors Office, Kemble St. to serve application. I spoke to Prachi Kanse who was surprised that I had made the application before receiving a response to my Pre-action letter dated 30th. November 2015. She asked me to wait; I waited for about 20 minutes and then she issued me with a letter responding to my letter dated 30th. November 2015. The letter she gave me was dated 22nd. December 2015.1 therefore assumed she had just written the letter. *(It appears I made the correct decision to visit the Court to avoid my application from being out of time)*

2/ 23rd.December 2015,1 sent an E.mail and recorded delivery letter to Administrative court explaining my experience at the court the previous day. Also, that I had been advised incorrectly, regarding the time scale for my application. *(No acknowledgement or response)*

3/ 8th. January 2016, received a report from Tim Buley (Barrister). The report was sent via. TSol.) Response to report 9th. January 2016 in the form of a letter by Mr. Richard Connaughton. *(No acknowledgement or response).* NOTE! Additional letters sent 9th February, 8th. March 2016.

4/ 25th. February 2016, received letter from GLD requesting payment of costs and enclosing a court order by Mrs. Justice Lang, dated 21st. January 2016. The order required a response within 14 days. (4th. February 2016) Note! Order not received until 25th. February 2016, 21days after expiry of date to respond. A response was sent to GLD 8th. March 2016

No acknowledgement or response).

A request was made by me to my solicitor to arrange a conference with a Barrister to discuss situation. Note! Solicitor did not arrange any conference.

5/ 24th. March 2016, received letter from GLD informing me that they had issued a letter to the Administrative Court informing them that they had made an error in the Court Order issued by Mrs. Justice Lang dated 21st. January 2016.

6/ 6th. April 2016 a letter to the Court was issued by Woodfines (Solicitors) informing them of the fundamental mistake made by Mrs. Justice Lang regarding the Court Order issued 21st. January 2016.

7/ 25th. April 2016, the Court responded to Woodfines (Solicitor) stating that the case had been referred back to

Mrs. Justice Lang for further consideration.

8/ 5th. May 2016, I sent a very long and comprehensive letter, including many informative documents (Evidence) to Mr. Martyne Cowlin (Admin Court).
Note! the letter was sent recorded delivery. *(No acknowledgment or response)*

9/ Friday 13th. May 2016,1 received an E.mail from Woodfines(Solicitor) informing me that an order had been issued by Mrs. Justice Lang dated 9th. May 2016. The order stated that I had 14 days to respond from 12th May 2016. (26th. May 2016).

10/ Monday 16th. May 2016,1 tried to contact Woodfines (Solicitor) to request them to respond to the order and was told the solicitor (Catherine Sandbach) was not available. I tried again everyday up to Friday 20th. May 2016 and was informed that the solicitor was not available. After insisting I spoke to someone, I spoke to Keith Jones (Partner) who informed me that the solicitor (Catherine Sandbach) had been withdrawn from my case, no reason was given.

11/ Because of the time scale, I Emailed and wrote to the Administrative Court 24th. May 2016. (Letter sent recorded delivery) requesting further time to respond to the order dated 9th. May 2016. *(No acknowledgement or response)*.

12/1 sent an E.mail to Woodfines(Solicitor) informing them of my dissatisfaction regarding the way my case was being conducted. I received an E.mail in response requesting me to inform the court that they no longer represent me. I tried to contact Keith Jones but was informed that he was not available. I sent an Email. Requesting them to inform me when and why, Catherine Sandbach was withdrawn from my case. *(No acknowledgement or response).*

13/ Because I had not received a response to my letter to the Court dated 24th. May 2016 I contacted the Post Office to see if my letter had been received, I was advised to contact the court. I telephoned the Administrative Court Office at 11.20am. 2nd. June 2016. After a very long wait I eventually spoke to a lady called Dorothy, she informed me that they had received my letter. I asked if she could read the contents of the letter to me; she requested me to stay on the line. I waited until 11.36am. when the line went dead. I redialed the number and again after a very long wait I made contact with Dorothy, she apologised and transferred me to the Case Progression Team, I eventually spoke to a lady called Momotaj. We had a long conversation and she eventually informed me that my case had been closed.

She also informed me that the court had sent an E.mail to Woodfine(Solicitors) on 26th. May 2016. (This Email had not been forwarded to me.). She kindly Emailed me a copy of the E.mail. Because I was very confused by the whole process, she informed me that I should make an application for the case to be renewed. She advised me that I should complete Form N244 and sent it with a cheque for £255.

14/ I received a letter from the court dated 1st. June 2016 informing me that my case had been closed.

15/ 5th. June 2016,1 sent a letter (Sent special delivery) (Received and signed for 8.11am. 7th. June 2016). My letter was addressed to Administrative Court. Explaining my concern about the manner in which my case is being conducted. I included 20 letters to confirm the information contained in my letter. *(No acknowledgement or response)*

16/ Letter sent to court 27th. June 2016, (special delivery) requesting information regarding previous letters and E.mails. *(No acknowledgement or response).*

17/ E.mail sent to Admin Court. 25th. July 2016, requesting response to communications.
(No acknowledgement or response)

18/ I received a letter from Kimberlie Eatough (Admin. Team Leader). 3rd. August 2016.

19/1 responded to Kimberlie Eatough 8th. August 2016. Letter and documents received and signed for 7.45am. 9th. August 2016. (By Jordon)

20/ Letter received from GLD. 15th. August 2016. requesting payment of costs. Letter from Richard Hilton.

21/ Letter sent to Prachi Kanse GLD. from Richard Connaughton dated 16th. August 2016.
(No acknowledgement or response)

22/ Mr. Connaughton sent a letter by E.mail to Ms. Kanse, 25th. August 2016.

23/ I received a response to my letter dated 8th. August 2016. The letter dated 30th. August 2016 was a very evasive letter from Geraint Evans (GLD). Informing me; that if I was not satisfied with the way my complaint has been dealt with. I should write to Communications and Customer

Services Team.

24/ I have written to Communications and Customer Service Team, informing them of my dissatisfaction at the manner in which my case has been conducted from the beginning, and have supplied them with many documents to support my complaint. 8th. September 2015.
Letter sent special delivery 10.19am 9th. September 2016. It was received and signed for by Peter 11.27am. 12th. September 2016. *(no acknowledgement or response)*

25/ Mr. Connaughton wrote to Prachi Kanse 15th. September 2016 referring to the 5 grounds which they consider "Unarguable and without merit",
(no acknowledgement or response)

26/ I again wrote to Communications and Customer Service Team Services Team (CCST) 29th. September 2016 enclosing document "J'accuse" and letter to GLD. (Sent special deliver)
(no acknowledgement or response)

27/ I received a typical evasive letter from Richard Redgrave (CCST) 30th. September 2016.

28/ I responded to Mr. Redgrave's letter 13th. October2016.1 commented on various points he had stated in his letter (30th. September 2016)

29/ Richard wrote a series of letters and Emails to Mr. Lee John-Charles head of Litigation Legal Dept. GLD. 1st, 4th, 8th,9th,11th. November 2016. *(no acknowledgement or response)*

30/ Richard wrote further letters to Lee John-Charles

21st. Nov 2016 and 7th. December 2016
   (no acknowledgement or response)

31/ HMCTS supplied incorrect information to Parliamentary Ombudsman regarding my case. (Letter dated 22nd. December 2016 from Parliamentary Ombudsman, received 27th. December 2016. Letter stated "we have decided to take no further action."

32/ Because of the Christmas period it was not possible to communicate with anyone. I eventually sent an Email, to Ms. Wright (PHSO) 3rd. January 2017 explaining that the Courts and the Inspectorate had supplied them with incorrect information.

33/ Richard Connaughton wrote a long informative letter to Ms. Wright (PHSO) 4th. January 2017, referring to the incorrect information they had received from Courts and Inspectorate. I again sent an Email. 6th. January 2017. *(no acknowledgement or response)*

34/ I received an Email from Ms. Wright (PHSO) informing me that she was on maternity leave and would not be responding to any communications.

35/ I wrote a long informative letter to Ms. Wright (PHSO) dated 11th. January 2017. Because I had been communicating with her previously.

36/1 wrote to Mr. Redgrave (HM Courts) 14th. January 2017 requesting him to respond, to various communications/correspondence, between us over the past weeks.

36/1 received a letter from Mr. Redgrave (HM Courts)

18th. January 2017. The letter was dated 12th. January 2017. The letter informed me that "I do not propose to comment further if you write again on this matter". And suggested I contact my MP to refer my case to Parliamentary Ombudsman (Which I have already done)

37/1 wrote a letter to PHSO 23rd. January 2017 addressed to Sir/Madam because I had not been informed who had replaced Ms. Wright. I also wrote to Nadine Dorries to keep her up to date with the situation.

38/ Mr. Connaughton wrote to Mr. Redgrave (HM. Courts) 25th. January 2017 informing him of his dissatisfaction at the treatment I had received from HM Courts and Tribunal Service.
No acknowledgement or response

39/1 again wrote to PHSO 26th. January 2017 enclosing the letter written by Mr. Connaughton.

40/ I contacted PHSO 3rd. February 2017 and spoke to Alec Fox who informed me that there was nothing further they could do. I eventually spoke to a lady called Janet in Customer Care who was most helpful. She advised me to complete certain forms which she would send to me to have my case reviewed. She phoned me later that day to inform me that her manager had looked at my case and it would be reviewed without completing any forms.

41/1 received an Enforcement order from Andrew Wilson & Co. High Court Enforcement. Dated 10th. February 2017. Relating to an order, issued by the High Court 21st. January 2016. I wrote to Andrew Wilson & Co. explaining that the order issued 21st. January 2016 giving me 14 days to respond, was not made available to me until

24th. February 2016 Therefore I was unable to contest it. The same Judge issued another Order dated 9th. May 2016 quashing the previous order because mistakes were made by the court and stated "costs reserved". I also contacted Richard Hilton (GLD) to discuss the situation. After a while he said "I am not prepared to spend any more time discussing this case" and put the phone down.

42/ Mr. Connaughton sent an Email to Prachi Kanse (GLD) 17th. February 2017. Regarding the enforcement order. I also wrote a letter to Mr. Lee John-Charles (GLD) 17th. February 2017 informing him of the situation and requested him to investigate my case.
(No acknowledgement or response)

43/ I contacted PHSO 20th. February 2017 and spoke to Phil Whitehead who informed me that my case is now being investigated by Mr. Mark Hair. I wrote to PHSO 24th. February 2017 informing them of what I had been advised.

44/ Mr. Connaughton sent an Email to Mr. John-Charles (GLD) 24th. February 2017 informing him of the situation, and that it was a case of "Misconduct in Public Office" which should be considered by the Metropolitan Police. He stated he was tired of the lawlessness and allowed 14 days to do what is right. *(No acknowledgement or response)*

45/I was visited by an Enforcement Officer 3rd. March 2017 relating to the Enforcement order issued 13th. February 2017.1 had no choice but to pay him. I made him aware of the situation and he advised me to contact the court and appeal.
46/ I hand delivered a letter and evidence to the Bedford

County Court 16th. March 2017 requesting "Judgement to be Set Aside" and "Stay of Writ".

47/1 received a response to my letter on 17th. March 2017, requesting me to comment on the contents of the letter.

48/ I hand delivered a letter to the Bedford County Court, 22nd. March 2017. The letter also contained various other documents to be considered.

49/ Letter to Mr. Lee John-Charles (GLD) 24th. April 2017, including request for costs *(No acknowledgement or response)*.

50/ Sent a letter to Prachi Kanse (GLD) 29th. April 2017, informing her of an incident concerning the mental state of my wife., caused by the actions of GLD. Received a response by Email. 3rd. May 2017 stating she would respond as soon as possible.

51/1 received a letter from Bedford Court 6th. May 2017, informing me that "The County Court can do nothing. It is a High Court matter. They also enclosed all the documents I had supplied them with. So now I have to apply to the High Court.

52/ 8th. May 2017,1 telephoned High Court for information. I spoke to a lady who was most helpful, and she said she would send me a pack which would explain everything I need to do.

53/ 9th. May 2017,1 received a large bundle from Civil Appeal Office as promised. I read contents, and because it is very complicated, I intend to attend RCJ to ask for assistance in completing the necessary forms to make my claim.

54/ Contacted RCJ and made appointment to attend Personal Support Unit (PSU) at 11.30am. Tuesday 16th. May

55/ Tuesday 16th. May 2017. I attended PSU at Royal Court. The following is a summary of my experience at Royal Courts of Justice.

ROYAL COURTS OF JUSTICE EXPERIENCE

On 16th. March 2017 I attended Bedford County Court to deliver an application to have a court order judgement issued January 2016 to be "Set aside". I received a letter from the court dated 17th. March 2017, requesting more information. The information was hand delivered to the court 22nd. March 2017. I received a letter from the court. 6th. May 2017 informing me that they could not help, and I should apply to the High Court.

I contacted the High Court 8th. May 2017 and spoke to a lady who was very pleasant and helpful. She informed me that I need to make an application using various forms. She kindly mailed the forms and guidance to me the next day. The forms appeared quite complicated. I contacted the High Court again, and was referred to the Personal Support Unit (PSU).

I arranged a meeting with PSU for 11.30am. Tuesday 16th. May 2017.

I travelled to Royal Courts of Justice, London, to attend the meeting. I was seen by a very pleasant and helpful lady named Hannah. We spent one and a half hours together where she advised me how to complete the forms and application. She advised me to go to the Fees Office to obtain an Exemption Certificate using form EX160. I attended the fees office in another part of the building and was issued with an Exemption Certificate. The people there were very helpful, and suggested I attend the Appeals Office in another part of the building to see if the Certificate was adequate for my purpose. The people at the Appeals Office who attended to me did not appear to understand what I required, and a senior officer directed me to "The Admin Office" in another part of the building. The girl who attended to me at the Admin. Office did not appear to know what I required; I supplied her with all the papers. Eventually she informed me that she would get a more senior person to attend to me. After some time another person attended to me. I understand the person was a "Case progression Officer". This person appeared very officious, and when I tried to explain the situation, she became very bureaucratic and attempted to talk over me. She appeared to be reluctant to listen, and understand what I was trying to explain to her. I realised I was not going to receive any assistance from her. I asked for her name; she said "why!". I said I need to know her name for my records, she reluctantly wrote her name on a scrap of paper. Because it was not very legible, I asked if she could spell it out for me. She said "We do not usually give out names".

I was quite frustrated and informed her that whenever I write to the Royal Courts Admin Office, I never receive any acknowledgement or response. She stated "We do not respond to letters".

It became obvious she wanted to end our conversation and wished to pull down the blind at the counter. I read the name she had written on the piece of paper and believe it read "Clodeagh O'Neill, Case Progression Office, Administrative Court."

I had travelled to Royal Courts of Justice in London, to seek assistance and advice; I spent three and a half hours going from one department to another. I have to say; most of the people I dealt with were courteous and helpful, however I was disappointed and frustrated at the service I received at the Administrative Office.

I am 78 years old, and do not enjoy travelling to London to seek assistance and advice. However, I felt I needed assistance, but, was disappointed at the way I was treated by Ms. O,Neill.

56/ 18th. May 2017 sent Email to Cloagh O'Neill (Admin office)

57/ 25th. May 2017 sent bundle to Civil Appeals Office regarding application for Judicial Review, including 3 copies of: N161 forms, Copies of Court orders, Remission Certificate, Summary of Events, Letter to Lee John-Charles GLD, Royal Courts of Justice experience   and E.mails to Ms .O'Neill.

58/ 6th. June 2017, I received a letter from Mr. John Hebden (Registry Office) HMCTS.   returning all the documents I had sent to the Court 25th. May 2017. I telephoned Mr. Hebden and asked him to explain the contents of his letter. I explained the situation and informed him of the information and advice I had received from the Administrative Court Office. He informed me that I had been given incorrect information and advised me to contact Admin. Office. Tel No. 02079476655

I telephoned Admin. Office and spoke to a very pleasant and helpful lady called Karen Welford. We had a long conversation and I explained the situation. She informed me that I had been misinformed by the Admin Office regarding the required forms to make an application. She explained that I need to make a new application using form N244 together with a completed EX160 form regarding fees. She advised me to complete the forms and send them with a letter explaining my situation, for her attention to Administrative Court Office, Royal Courts of Justice, Strand, London, WC2A 2LL. She also advised me that if I wished to make a complaint, I should write to Sana Gilani her office manager.

59/ 10th. June 2017, sent letter to Karen Wellford (RCJ) and included completed forms N244 and EX160 and various documents to support my Application Notice.

60/ Note; I sent a letter to Prachi Kanse 9/4/17. Received E.mail response 3/5/17 stating "Will respond as soon as possible". Sent Email 2/6/17 asking for response. Received E.mail response 8/6/17, stating "I hope to respond shortly". Sent another E.mail 14/6/17 asking "How long do you require to respond?"

61/ Received letter from Admin Court dated 16th. June 2017 including sealed application using form N244.

62/ 20th. June 2017 served sealed application on CBC and GLD.

63/ 21st. June 2017, Received an Email response from Prachi Kanse in response to my letter dated 9th. April 2017 and subsequent follow up Emails.

64/ Sent letter and enclosed letter to Karen Wellford (Admin Court) 24th. June 2017.

65/ 9th. July 2017, I sent letter and information to Admin. Court; also, letter to Sana Gilani (Office manager) (See below)

Alan. J. Bowers
Ein-Ty, 123b Clophill Rd. Maulden, Beds. MK45 2AE
Tel. 01525 860036 E.mail. bowers-alan(q),sky.com

9th. July 2017

Administrative Court Royal Courts of Justice The Strand London WC2A 2LL

Ref. CO6548/2015
Ref. Z1530338/PNK/B5

Dear Sir/Madam

I refer to a letter **Ref. Z1530338/PNK/B5 sent to you by Ellen Richardson (For the Treasury Solicitor) dated 6th. July 2017. (Copy enclosed) the letter relates to an application using forms N244 and other documents sent to you 10th. June 2017. The application was duly sealed (14th. June 2017) and returned to me. Copies of the sealed applications were served upon Central Bedfordshire Council (CBC), and Government Legal Department (GLD) 20th. June 2017.**

I wish to make you aware of misleading statements, and untruths contained within the letter to the court, in an attempt to "pervert the course of justice."

I will comment on the false information within the letter

using the following bullet points.

- **The January 2016 Order**
Reference to order issued by Mrs. Justice Lang dated 21st. January 2016. Order states [sent to Claimant, Defendant, and any interested parties 2nd. February 2016.] This order was not made available to me (Claimant) until 25th. February 2016. [9 days after the time allowed to respond]. *"Owing to an administrative or postal error"* as quoted by Justice Lang (9th.April 2016).
Paragraph 4: Refers to letter written by GLD to court dated 24th. March 2016. (Enclosed) (2) This letter was prompted by a letter written to GLD by Mr. Connaughton dated 8th. March 2016 (Enclosed). (3). GLD were informed that incorrect information had been provided to the court by the GLD lawyer relating to Judicial and Statutory Review.
On being informed of the misleading and incorrect information provided by the GLD lawyer, Mrs Justice Lang issued a new order dated 9th. May 2016, completed 12th. May 2016. (Copy enclosed) (4) Order states "Costs reserved" and 14 days to respond. The order also states "Ought to be considered by another judge".

- **The May 2016 Order.**
Paragraph 1. Letter states "The claimant appears to have instructed solicitors in around April 2016" I first instructed my solicitor 14th. July 2014 concerning my case and made them aware of my dealings with Admin Court and application for Judicial Review 29th. December 2015. Paragraph 4. [The May order was sent to parties on 12th. May 2016.] I received no order until informed by my solicitor by Email 13th. May 2016 that the order had been issued. I tried to contact my solicitor Monday 16th. May 2016, (Earliest opportunity). I tried every day until Friday

20th. May 2016 and was informed they would contact me. Eventually, I was informed that the solicitor concerned had been taken of the case and had left their employment. Because, of the timescale to respond (26th. May 2016), I responded myself on 24th. May 2016; by Email and recorded delivery mail, (copies enclosed)

NOTE! I had no acknowledgement or response.

Despite many attempts to contact Admin Court for a response, I eventually spoke to a very pleasant lady called Momotaj 2nd. June 2016 who informed me that because I had not responded in time to the court my case had been closed. This was confirmed in a letter dated 1st. June which I received 2nd June 2016. Because I was confused and concerned about the actions of Admin Court, I sent a very informative letter enclosing 20 documents to the Admin. Court 5th. June 2016 (Copy enclosed)

NOTE! I have also enclosed an Email from Clodagh O,Neil (Admin Office) which confirms the admin office did receive my Email and letter 24th. May 2016. She denied it when I spoke to her during my visit to the admin office 16th. May 2017. See copy of Email sent to her 18th. May 2017 (Enclosed).!

- **Enforcement of Costs Order.**
Letters dated 25th. February 2016; 15th. August; 21st.September2016 also response to letter dated 15th. August. Enclosed. No record of letter dated 28th. October 2016.

Please see enclosed letter to Andrew Wilson & Co. dated 15th. February 2017 referring to "Notice of Enforcement" explaining the situation. Also letter to Mr. John-Charles (GLD) from Mr. Connaughton 23rd. March 2017 referring to my case.

I was obliged to pay the Enforcement Officer 7th. March 2017; when I informed him of the situation he advised me

67

to contest the order. (I realise he is not qualified to make such a statement). However, I have been trying to contest the order since (Trying to obtain justice) **SEE!** "Summary of Events regarding Application for Judicial Review" enclosed

- **The Application**

Paragraph 1. The order issued 9th. May 2016 clearly states *"Costs reserved"* and acknowledges that she acted upon incorrect information she had received from the GLD lawyer with respect to the order she issued 21st. January 2016. The Judge also allowed me 14

days in which to request my application be reviewed; and that it should be considered by another Judge.
Although my application to review the application was made within the timescale allowed 26th. May 2016. (Which the Admin office refutes) the court closed my case.

Paragraph 2. My application for Judicial Review has not been determined. The case has been closed based upon untruthful statements that I did not respond within the time allowed. Proof of the true situation is evidenced within the documents enclosed. Therefore, my case for Judicial Review is ongoing.

Paragraph 4. The trail of Emails referred 16th. August 2016 (Enclosed) confirm that GLD is rather confused and still suffers from communication problems.

Paragraph 5. GLD states that my application to "Set aside" Justice Lang's decision 21st. January 2016 is significantly late and unsubstantiated. It is because of the errors and misleading information provided by GLD in the first instant. (As stated by Judge). It has been stated by GLD that they provided incorrect information to the court.

With respect to Reason Two; GLD has been requested many times to state why the 5 initial grounds were unarguable and without merit, in their opinion. Again, GLD are stating that although I was allowed 14 days to respond; I failed to do so. The evidence provided proves that they are being economical with the truth.

Paragraph 6. With reference to the 5 grounds, these were explained in great detail by Mr. Connaughton in his letter to Prachi Kanse (GLD) in a letter dated 9th. January 2016. (Copy enclosed).

CONCLUSION.

As explained above, the GLD are content in continuing to pervert the course of justice, by using every means possible to prevent the actions and conduct of an Inspector directed by the Secretary of State DEFRA (Mr. Peter Millman) from appearing before an independent court of law. My application cannot be determined by reference to papers but requires the full application and case to be determined by a fair and impartial court of law.

....

With my application sent 10th. June 2017,1 enclosed other documents for you to consider.

I have been fighting my case for justice for 26 years and have been trying to get my case heard before your court since 22nd. December 2015Again I refer you to document "Summary of Events regarding Application for Judicial Review"

Although I am now 78 years old, I am only now beginning to unbelievably understand and experience the Misconduct and Malfeasance which is so blatant within some Government Departments and associated authorities. To illustrate this, I have enclosed a further factual and informative document written by Mr. Richard Connaughton.

I have also enclosed a document entitled "J'accuse" which reveals the malfeasance. within many authorities.
NOTE!

Because the Administrative Office (RCJ) and GLD appear to experience difficulties regarding the sending and receiving of correspondence, I will send this information by special delivery.

Yours sincerely,

Alan Bowers
Enclosed; 15 documents.

Sent special delivery mail.
....

66/ 4th. August 2017. I received a plain brown envelope with handwritten address through the mail; it contained one piece of paper. The piece of paper was a court order.

from John Howell QC. (Deputy judge at High Court) no other information was included.

67/ 11th. August 2017, Richard Connaughton wrote a letter to John Howell QC. and included various documents. (J'accuse II, and memorandum to John Charles (GLD) See copy.

11 August 2017

Judge John Howell QC
Deputy High Court Judge
The High Court of Justice Queen's Bench Division
The Strand
London, WC2A 2LL   Your Reference: CO/6548/2015

My name is Richard Connaughton, superannuated soldier representing 78 year old Alan Bowers.

He has no money. His entire life's savings have been lost on the opposed defence of his home.

I need to know upon what evidence you depended in coming to your Decision promulgated on 3 August 2017 that Mr Bowers' submission is 'wholly without merit', and which appears at p.3 of the enclosed memorandum.

Thanking you in anticipation I am respectfully, Yours sincerely,

Richard Connaughton

Enclosures
A. *J'accuse II, Bowers Case III.*
B. Memorandum to John-Charles dated 8 August 2017.

68/ 14th. August 2017 I sent a copy of "J'accuse II" and a covering letter to the following: Judge John Howell; Mr. Haire PHSO; Susan Parton Legal Ombudsman; Rozina Sabour Telegraph; Nadine Dorries MP; Simon Colton QC; Michael Gove MP; ITV News Desk; Robin Stone Police; BBC Panorama; Watchdog; all by recorded delivery. I also sent copy (1st Class) to Malcolm Tattersall;

and hand delivered copy to Sarah Cox Beds, on Sunday.

69/ 15ᵗʰ. September 2017. Richard Connaughton presented a Report and covering letter to Mr. William Cooper, Admin Office, in answer to a request from Mr. Cooper. (See Report)

70/ 19ᵗʰ. September 2017,1 sent a copy of Richards Report to:

LIST OF PEOPLE TO BE SENT RICHARDS REPORT TO COURT.

Nadine Dorries:
Nadine Dorries MP, House of Commons, London,SW1A OAA; William.Joce@pariliament.uk Tel; 02072195928, 02072195586

Legal Ombuds.Man:
Susan Parton, Legal Ombudsman, PO Box 6806, Wolverhampton,WV1 9WJ; 0121 2453305; Susan.Parton@Legalombudsman.org.uk

Parli. Ombuds.
PHSO, Millbank Towers, Millbank, London, SW1P 4QP; Te. 03450154033; phso.enquires@ombudsman.org.uk Case No. F0000561

Telegraph:
Rozinor Sabour, News Desk, Telegraph, 111 Buckingham Palace Rd. London, SW1W ODT Tel;02079312541, M. 0770832489: Rozina.sabour@telegraph.co.uk
Police:
Robin Stone, Investigating Officer 8177, Beds, Cambs, Herts. Police Professional Standards Dept. Biggleswade

Police Station, Station Rd. Biggleswade, Beds. SG1 8
8AL; Tel.01234 842604: Case No. CO/00410/17,
Robin.Stone2@cambs.pnn.police.uk

Karen Jones:
c/o Zoe Bluck, Tanfield Chambers, 2-5 Warwick Court,
London, WC1R 5DJ; Tel. 02074215300,
KarenJones@tanfieldchambers.co.uk:
ZoeBluck@tanfieldchambers.co.uk

Malcolm Tattersall;
58 Bedford St. Ampthill, Beds. MK45 2NB ; Tel.
07787502171; mal.tattersal@me.com

Beds, on Sun.
49 Mill St. Bedford, MK40 3EU. Liz Farrel,
bussinessservices@lsnmedia.co.uk Te;

Times &Citizen:
News Desk, Times & Citizen, 3 Northouse, Bond Ave.,
Bletchley, MK1 1SW. Tel;.01908 371133
editorial@timesandcitizen.co.uk

Paul Duckett;
81 Oliver St. Ampthill, Beds. MK45 2SA; Tel.07988184061.
paul.duckett@centralbedfordshire.gov.uk

Mike Blair;
mike.blair@centralbedfordshire.gov.uk 4, Lyme Rd.
Ampthill, Beds. MK45 2LB. Tel. 03003008561

Supporters
Rights of way sufferers

Watchdog:

Watchdog, 1st Floor, BBC Dock House, Media City UK, Salford, M50 2HL; watchdog@bbc.co.uk

Panorama: BBC Panorama, Zone D, 4th. Floor, BBC Broadcasting House, Portland Place, London, W1A 1AA, panorama.reply@bbc.co.uk

Anglia News.
News Desk, ITV Anglia, Norwich, NR1 3JG.
anglianews@itv.com Judge Ayres (Bedford)
Brian Reardon

71/ Report of Telephone Conversation to Admin Court 10.00am 25th. September 2017

I telephoned Admin Court at 10.00am Monday 25th. September 2017; no one answered until 10.20am.

The lady who answered was Dorothy Amoah. I asked for the extension No. for Mr. William Cooper I was informed that they could not supply that information. The lady said "I will put you through"... After sometime I was informed he was not available. I requested to speak to Karen Welford.... after sometime I was informed she was not available, because she was at the desk. I requested to speak to Sana Gilani, after some time I was informed that she was not available.

However, Dorothy appeared to know what my call was about, and informed me that a letter had been sent by Mr. Ian Carr to Mr. Connaughton regarding the matter, and was posted 21st. September 2017. Mr. Connaughton received the letter Monday 25th. September 2017. The letter was the usual nonsensical letter you usually receive.

Alan Bowers
Ein-Ty 123B Clophill Rd.

CHAPTER IX

"IS JUSTICE JUST A WORD"

FORWORD

"Justice is a concept on ethics and law that means that people behave in a way that is fair, equal and balanced for everyone"

....

This is a story about "The struggle for JUSTICE"

PREFACE

During the early parts of our life we are taught to Respect and Accept many things that will affect us during our lives.

It could be: Religion, Education; Medical; Politics; Laws; etc.

There are of course, many learned and devoted people within these particular subjects who are dedicated, truthful, and sincere.

However, as we progress though life, we discover by experience, that not all is as we expected.

I consider myself to be a normal law-abiding citizen with certain standards which I endeavor to uphold.

Over the past 27 years I have experienced much distress and financial burden attributed to the actions of some, who we would expect to be Truthful, Lawful, and Sincere, whilst acting out the particular positions they hold.

Recently I have produced a book called "The Path & I" which tells in great detail the distress I and my family have experienced through the actions of those who "Derive pleasure at the distress of others "

This document "Justice what Justice" reveals the Malfeasance and Malicious actions of a company of Solicitors in whom I placed my trust to obtain Justice.

NOTE; All documents, files etc. referred to in "Justice what Justice" are available within my files

Index

CHAPTER: I Justice what Justice

Because of the malicious and unacceptable actions of Central Bedfordshire Council (CBC), regarding a public Footpath that had been imposed upon my property in 1997 had caused me and my family, many years of distress and financial burden, I sought the advice of a local solicitor (Woodfines of Bedford).

I wished to enquire into the possibility of referring the actions of CBC to the Courts regarding "Misconduct in Public Office".

I first attended Woodfines Bedford Office 2nd. July 2014 where I met Catherine Sandbach (Litigation Solicitor). We spent a few hours discussing my case and I produced many documents to illustrate my claim.

I received a letter from Woodfins dated 18th. July 2014, the letter set out my intentions and was requested to pay £234 for them to investigate my case.

Ms. Sandbach informed me that the details of my claim would be investigated by their Litigation Team to access the strength of my case.

On 3rd. September 2014 I sent an E.mail to Woodfines informing them of the recent actions of CBC when they withdrew a Section 116 WCA from the court which was due to take place 8th, 9th, 10th. September 2014, at Luton Magistrates Court.

The Section 116, was presented to the Court by CBC. 13th. June 2013. The case was to be heard 17th. July 2013. On the day CBC requested an Adjournment. The case was adjourned until 2nd. January 2014. The CBC. attended and requested a 2nd. Adjournment. The case was adjourned until 8th, 9th, 10th. September 2014.

The CBC requested a further adjournment 21st. August 2014. The Court refused their application. In desperation CBC withdrew the Section 116 application from the Court 2nd. September 2014.

After receiving this information, Woodfines sent me an E.mail 4th. September 2014 stating *"It seems to me that their actions could continue to build your potential case for misfeasance in public office in relation to the ongoing actions   of the council and its officers"*.

During September 2014 I delivered more documents and evidence to Woodfines

I received a letter from Ms. Sandbach 4th. November 2014 stating that Woodfines are prepared to enter into "Conditional Fee Agreement" (CFA).

I attended their office in Bedford 10th. November 2014 where, we both signed a "Conditional Fee Agreement", I also suppled them with a very detailed dossier relating to "Misconduct in Public Office" to present to their barrister. Ms. Sandbach sounded very positive and indicated the case would be presented to CBC by the end of the year 2014.

I sent an E.mail to Ms. Sandbach 23rd. November attaching a copy of a letter I had sent to the Inspectorate 21st. November 2014 illustrating the Misconduct of CBC and others.

I wrote a letter to Chief Executive, (CBC) 14th. February 2015, illustrating the corruption within his authority, and sent a copy to Woodfines (received no acknowledgement).

I made several calls to Woodfines enquiring about my case. Each time they apologised for not contacting me. I eventually received an E.mail 1st. April 2015 from Cristopher Northway (Trainee solicitor) stating. *"Catherine is continuing to liaise with the barrister in this matter, and will provide you with a comprehensive update after Easter"*.

I attended the Bedford office 14th. April 2015 where Catherine informed me that   she was still waiting for a response from the barrister. While I was there, she endorsed a letter (Signed and stamped) which I had written to the

Planning Inspectorate.

I received an E.mail from Catherine Sandbach 1st. May 2015 informing me that she had referred my case to a different barrister, and hoped to have an opinion by Mid. May.

I received an E.mail from Catherine 17th. July 2015 requesting me to supply further information for the barrister to consider. I hand delivered the requested information 20th. May 2015.

Despite many attempts to contact Woodfines I received an E.mail 19th. October 2015 from Catherine informing me of the barrister's opinion regarding my case. (Not very positive). I requested a copy of the barrister's report and received a copy early in November 2015

I attended the Bedford office 23rd. November 2015 and discussed the situation with Catherine. I supplied a letter and a comprehensive dossier which included details and information concerning a public Inquiry which took place September 2015.1 also informed Catherine that I would be applying for Judicial Review, and requested they represent me.

I attended the Bedford office 29th. December 2015 and discussed the situation with Catherine and informed her of the present situation regarding my application for Judicial Review. **NOTE:** *She did not appear to be au-fait with the procedure.*

I hand delivered a bundle for the attention of Catherine to the Bedford office 15th. *January 2016.*

I met with Catherine 29th.February 2016 to discuss the situation, and agreed to instruct a barrister, and to respond to a letter I had received from Government Legal Department (GLD). We also agreed it would be appropriate to have a conference with the barrister.

I sent an Email. To Catherine 10th. March 2016 with an attachment (a letter to GLD dated 8th. March 2016). I also requested an update on the proceedings.

I received an Email. From Catherine 24th.March 2016 informing me she would out of the office for the Easter break. She also informed me that the barrister she had contacted would not be available until the latter part of April and asked if I wished to look for another Counsel.

I received an Email. 4th. April 2016 from Catherine informing me that they propose to send a letter to the Royal Courts of Justice in response to information received from the court, which indicated the statement made by the Judge to be incorrect and asked that they reconsider my application for Judicial Review.

I sent an Email. to Catherine 25th. April 2016 informing her that I had received an Email. from Prachi Kanse (GLD) in forming me that the Judge had made an error in her decision regarding my application for Judicial Review.

I received an Email. 27th. April 2016 from Catherine attaching a letter they had received from GLD which stated that the papers had been referred back to the Judge for further consideration.

I receive an Email. Friday 13th. May 2016 from Sarah Craddock (Legal Secretary Litigation) in the name of Catherine Sandbach with an attachment from the Court granting 14 days in which to renew (review) my application for Judicial Review. She also states.

"Accordingly, this would be a good time for us to put all of the information together in one place for them to determine whether permission should be allowed. I am forwarding this to the clerks for barrister in order to press them for an urgent conference in light of this so that we can get his input before anything is put together. If he is not available within this time, I will ask for an alternative barrister to provide advice.

NOTE: This is the time when things appear to

become mysteriously disconnected regarding Catherine Sandbach.

WHAT HAPPENED to CATHERINE SANDBACH?

I tried to contact Catherine Sandbach first thing Monday 16th. May 2016, and was told she was not available, and that I would be contacted later. I tried every day up to Friday 20th. 2016 and was told she is not available. I insisted that I spoke to someone, and eventually spoke to Keith Jones a Senior Partner of (Woodfines Solicitors). Mr. Jones informed me that Catherine Sandbach had been withdrawn from my case. He would not explain why.

I received an E.mail. from Mr. Jones 20th. May 2014 in which he informed me of certain barristers and recommended Kate Oiley. He requested me to phone him Monday 23rd. May 2016.

I telephoned Mr. Jones 23rd. May 2016 in the morning; I expressed my dissatisfaction at the manner in which Woodfines had conducted my case. I received an E.mail. from Mr. Jones 15:06 23rd. May 2016. Setting out different proposals and requested £5000 before continuing my case.

Because I only had a few days to respond to the court (26th. May 2016), I took it upon myself to respond. I sent a letter by E.mai 11:04 24th. May 2016. I also sent the letter by recorded mail 12:47.1 also sent an E.mail 10:18 24th. May 2016 to Mr. Jones, informing him of my actions and my dissatisfaction at the service I had received from Woodfines

I received an E.mail from Sarah Cradock (Woodfines 12:08. 24th. May 2016 requesting me to complete an attached form.

The form was to be sent to the Court informing them that Woodfines no longer acted for me.

I sent an E.mail 26th. May 2016 (12:27) to Mr. Jones informing him that I had tried to contact him, but was told he was not available. I also wished to know **Why** and **When** Catherine Sandbach was withdrawn from my case. I also informed him that because of my dissatisfaction with Woodfine's, and because of the time factor I had contacted the Court directly regarding my request for Judicial Review.

NOTE; I had discovered that Catherine Sandbach ceased to be employed by Woodfines(Solicitors). I have enquired when and why she left their employment.

I received a further E.mail 26th. May 2016(12:59) attaching an E.mail they had received from the court (11:22), They also threatened me with costs of £500 if I did not send a copy of the form they had sent me 24th. May 2016.1 sent an E.mail in return (17:0) stating that I would send a completed form to the court and GLD as soon as possible.

I informed Mr. Jones 27th. May 2016 that I had sent the completed forms and sent him a copy for his information.

On the same day 26th. May 2016 12:58, Mr. Jones through Ms. Eagle sent an E.mail to the Court attempting to explain the situation. The final paragraph of the E.mail. states *"If the court feels able to declare of its own motion that we are not the claimant's solicitors on the record that would be very helpful in all the circumstances"*

I sent an E.mail to Ms. Eagle(Legal Secretary) 31st. May 2016 requesting that in view of the fact I no longer wished Woodfines to represent me, to arrange for me to collect all documents/evidence I had supplied regarding my case.

I received a letter from the Court 1st. June 2016 (From A. Lee Senior Operations Manager) informing me (*Leave to apply for Judicial Review has been refused and notice of that refusal was served upon the claimant on 05/02/2016.*

No request to reconsider the decision at the hearing has been lodged by the claimant within the period prescribed by the Civil Procedure Rule 54.12(4). Accordingly, I write to inform you that the file in this matter has been closed)

The information in this letter is untrue and refers to a different appeal?????.

I wrote to the Court 5th June 2016 informing the court of their incorrect information and the Maladministration of Woodfines (Solicitors). I Stated;

"Because of the confusion and mistakes made by the Court regarding my application for Judicial Review made 22nd. December 2015, and because of the Maladministration of my solicitors (Woodfines) I find myself in a very difficult and unacceptable position. Therefore, for Justice to be seen to be done. I request that my case be reviewed (not renewed), and all the evidence be reconsidered. I believe I have adhered to the correct procedure; it is because of the mistakes made by the Court and others that we have arrived at the present situation" I also supplied 20 letters/documents for consideration. I received a letter 28th. June 2016 from Mr. Jones (Solicitor) enclosing an Invoice for £6139.20.

I wrote a letter 11th. July 2016 to Mr. Jones again requesting information regarding the reason Catherine Sandbach had been withdrawn from my case; and why I was not informed, despite the many occasions I had tried to contact her. I also informed him that I contested the contents of the Invoice sent to me 28th. June 2016.

I received a response from Mr. Jones 13th. July 2016 endeavouring to answer my questions regarding Catherine Sandbach. He also requested me to pay for the services of Mr. Feldman (Barrister) who they had instructed. He also informed me that they would not release the documents I had requested.

I responded to Mr. Jones 21st. July 2016 and made several comments. I again informed Mr. Jones that because of the action or non-action of their company I had been subjected to much distress and unnecessary action. I also informed him that I had evidence of previous "Professional Misconduct" regarding Woodfmes (Solicitors)

I received a letter 25th. July 2016 from Sarah O'Brian (Trainee legal Executive, Woodfines) informing me that Mr. Jones was not available, and it would be inappropriate to address the points raised in my letter dated 22nd. July 2016 (should be 21st. July).

I received a letter 3rd. August 2016 from Mr. Jones attempting to respond to some of my concerns. He also threatened me with further action if I did not respond by 10th. August 2016

I received a letter 17th. August 2016 from Denise Turner (Credit Controller, Woodfmes) stating the balance of the Invoice could be subject to interest at the rate of 8.5% per. annum.

After seeking advice. I was advised to contact The Legal Ombudsman at PO Box 6806, Wolverhampton, WV1 9WJ.

I wrote to The Legal Ombudsman 28th. September 2016; explaining my situation and enclosed many documents. I received a response from Legal Ombudsman 14th. October 2016 supplying me with a Case No. CMP-046872.

I received an Enforcement Notice 13th. January 2017 from an address in Croydon referring to a Court Order issued in Salford (Manchester), and a notice from a Court in Oldham (Lancs). **NOTE:** I had no knowledge of these orders. These orders were made by Woodfines relating to an Invoice presented to me June 2016, which I had contested. After many hours on the phone and various investigations, I was advised to present certain forms and letters explaining the true situation. I eventually received an order to attend a hearing at

Bedford County Court 14th. February 2017.

I hand delivered a formal Letter of Complaint to Woodfines, 7th. February 2017 as instructed by The Legal Ombudsman.

I received an E.mail from Claire Potter (Woodfines) 9th. February 2017 stating that they had considered my case, and agreed to *"Set aside the Judgement against you and to stay the writ of execution"* whilst they consider my complaint letter of 7th. February 2017. She also requested me to sign a Consent Order which she had attached. She added that after the order had been signed, they would file it with the court prior to the hearing 14th. February 2017 so that the hearing could be vacated.

I received a phone call from Woodfines 6.20pm 9th. February 2017 asking me to sign the form and send it to them. I informed them that I had no intention of signing the form and would be attending the hearing, (they did not appear to be happy with my intentions).

I received a letter dated 10th. February 2017 from Adrian Frost (Client Care Partner) Woodfines. He stated my Complaints Letter dated 7th. February 2017 had been passed to him. He advised me that he would investigate and get back to me within the timeframe of the firms "Internal Complaints Procedure"

I sent an E.mail to Ms.Potter 12th. February 2017 informing her that I intend to attend the hearing 14th. February and state my case. I received a telephone call early Monday 13th. February 2017 from Mr. Keith Jones (Woodfines), he informed me that if I signed the form, there would be no need to attend the hearing. I advised him that I had every intention of attending the hearing. He shouted *"We will see you in court"* and put down the phone.

I attended the Court hearing at Bedford Court Tuesday 14th, February 2017.

See details of my attendance

Could this be the shortest Court Hearing?
Alan Bowers

I was directed by Bedford County Court to attend a Court Hearing at 10.0am Tuesday 14th. February 2017.

I attended the Court at St.Paul's Square Bedford.

I entered the building at 9.55am. And was directed to an office at the rear of the building, which meant I had to leave the building and walk around to the rear of the building to access the office.

After going through security, I presented the order to the court officer at 10.07am.

I was informed that the case had already been held and judgement had been made at 10.0am.

The case was concerning a court order issued by Woodfines (Solicitors) Bedford, against me for £7053.57; which I wished to contest.

The court officer informed me that a representative for Woodfines had attended earlier, and the case had been dealt with.

I requested to see the Judge. The officer accompanied me to a room to see the Judge. I asked the Judge (Judge Ayres) to explain the situation to me. He was very pleasant, and stated. "Woodfines attended earlier and judgement has been made to [set aside judgement and to stay the writ].". I was very confused and asked "How long did it take" he replied "Twenty seconds". I could not understand the situation, and enquired, how could a decision be made without me being present.

He said *"Mr. Bowers do not worry, it has all been sorted, and you will no longer be pursued regarding this matter"*. I had to accept what he stated, but I informed him that I wished to make a counter claim against Woodfines; for the distress and financial burden they had imposed upon me.

He informed me that *"Woodfines and you should get your heads together".*

NOTE:

Woodfines have been representing me in an attempt to bring an action against Central Bedfordshire Council for Misconduct and Malfeasance. We had a "No Win no Fee" agreement made 10th. November 2014. Also, in my attempt to obtain a Judicial Review, against a decision made by a Government Inspector. Over that period they have been most unprofessional and did not appear to be familiar with the proceedings. I have requested the Legal Ombudsman to investigate the conduct and actions of Woodfines (Solicitors).

I received another letter from Adrian Frost 16th, February' 2017 stating he had investigated the file and requested that I should arrange a meeting with him and Keith Jones regarding my concerns.

I wrote to the Legal Ombudsman 20th. February 2017 informing him of recent events and repeated my request to investigate the conduct and actions of Woodfines (Solicitors).

I received a Judgement Order from High courts of Justice BEDFORD 22nd. February 2017 informing me that,

1/ Judgement had been set aside.

2/ Writ had been stayed.

3/ There be no order for costs.

I also received a letter from Land Registry dated. 20th. February 2017, informing me that Woodfins had cancelled the application to enter a restriction on my property,

I wrote to the Legal Ombudsman 24th. February 2017, informing them of recent events and supplied them with a copy of my "Summary of events concerning Woodfines Solicitors"

I wrote to Adrian Frost (Woodfmes) 25th. February 2017 in response to his letter date 16th. February 2017. I informed him that I agree in principle to a meeting with Woodfmes and put various questions to him.

I sent an E.mail to Woodfme's informing them that because I had not received an acknowledgement or response to my letter dated 25th. February 2017,1 intend to take further action if I do not receive a response within 3 days.

I received an E.mail from Malcolm Tattersall a freelance journalist. 3rd. March 2017. He had contacted Woodfines regarding my case, and asked many questions. Woodfines gave a negative response.

See details of questions and answers below!

Details of Questions and answers:
Mr. Tattersall wrote:
Hello,

I am a freelance journalist and have recently been talking to Mr. Alan Bowers, who at one time you were acting for in his legal fight over a disputed footpath, (the now notorious "Footpath 28") across his land in Maulden.

He claims that your firm agreed to take on his case under a Conditional Fee Agreement after telling him he had a strong case, but then suddenly out of the blue sent him a bill for nearly £7000.

Mr. Bowers is quite upset over what he considers rather shabby treatment by your firm. However, of course there are two sides to every story. So in the interests of fairness, I am contacting you to ask if you would please tell me:

1/ Why *and when was your solicitor Catherine Sandbach, who had been dealing with Mr. Bowers, suddenly withdrawn from the case? Mr. Bowers claims that although he asked for a reason, senior partner Keith Jones would not tell him.*

2/ When did Ms. Sandbach leave Woodfine's employment? Specifically, was this   on or before May 20 2016?

3/ Why was Mr. Bowers subsequently sent a bill for £7053.57 when he and Woodfines had signed a conditional fee agreement?

4/ Why did you then apply to a judge in Greater Manchester, some 160 miles away, for a court order against Mr. Bowers?

5/ Would it not have been easier, and perhaps more sensible, when all the parties involved were based in Bedfordshire, to apply to the court in Bedford, Luton, or even Milton Keynes?

6/ Is it also true that Mr. Bowers was not informed in advance of the court hearing so that he was able to argue his case and defend himself?

7/ Why did you then apply to the Land Registry for an interim charge on Mr. Bowers ' home in Maulden?

8/ Why if Mr. Bowers really did owe this quite sizeable sum, did Woodfine's then agree to "set aside judgement and stay the writ" against him after he objected in a most vociferous manner and threaten to complain to the Legal Ombudsman about the way he had been treated?

I am sure you would wish to comment on such matters before any article is published, so I would be grateful if you could come back to me asap - even if only, or whatever reason, to say "No comment".

Should you wish to discuss this over the phone or in your office, then please Get in touch. My mobile number is

Thanks,

Malcolm Tattersail.

Mr. Jones responded by Email. 2:35 Mar. 3. 2017.

Dear Mr. Tattersail,
Thank you for the below Email, which has been referred to me, since my name is mentioned.
Your query appears to relate to someone whom you believe to be a client of this firm.
As a journalist, you will be doubtless aware that if Mr. Bowers were or had been a client, I would not permitted by rules of professional conduct to respond to your query.
Kind regards Keith Jones.

Mr. Tattersall responded 3:17 March 3, 2017.

Thanks Mr. Jones. I will say in my article that you were given the opportunity to respond but replied "No comment"
Mai Tattersall

I received a letter 9th. March 2017 from Mr. Frost (Woodfines) dated 7th. March 2017. The letter was in response to my letter dated 25th. February 2017 in which   Mr. Frost made a vague attempt to answer the questions in my letter.

I responded to Mr. Frost's letter dated 7th. March 2017 on 12th. March 2017. I set out my thoughts, regarding his evasive answers to various questions. I also informed him that because of ongoing investigations and because all evidence had been collated, I could see no useful purpose in a meeting; unless they had any positive thoughts on how to reconcile my concerns. I further informed him that I intend to pursue the matter through the Legal Ombudsman and other avenues. I stated that if they wished to respond to my letter, I would be prepared to listen to avoid any unpleasantness.
On 12th. March 2017 I also sent a letter to the Legal Ombudsman informing them of events and enclosed copies of

correspondence between Woodfines and myself. I also enclosed a very informative letter written by Mr. Connaughton to Dorset Police (CID) which made reference to my case.

I received a letter from Mr. Frost (Woodfines) 23rd. March 2017. The letter was in response to my letter dated 12th. March 2017. At the end of the letter he states *"'If we do not hear nothing by 10th. April 2017, we shall continue with proceedings in respect of our unpaid costs".*

Mr. Connaughton wrote a long response to Woodfines 31st. March 2017, requesting answers to previous questions. I received an E.mail 4th. April 2017 from Mr. Frost regarding letter from Mr. Connaughton. ....

I responded to Mr. Frost's E.mail 5th. April 2017.

See letter written by Richard Connoughton

31 March 2017

Adrian Frost
Woodfines Solicitors
6 Bedford Road Sandy,
Beds
SG191EN

afrost@woodfmes.co.uk

Dear Mr Frost,

THE BOWERS CASE

I have seen your letter ANF/SW/BO/083499-0001 dated 23 March 2017 and have been invited by Mr Bowers to comment.

Your Ms Sandbach had been an occasional legal representative on Mr Bowers' behalf. He arranged for her to intercede with the High Court in respect of the Planning Court Order dated 21 January 2016 with a date of service of 2 February 2016. The Judge had been misdirected in so far as she described his application for judicial review as 'an abuse of process'. He should, she said, have commenced with an application for statutory review. The Judge was wrong in law: Mr Bowers was correct. At Mr Bowers' behest, your Ms Sandbach conveyed that information to the Judge.

In her Order dated 9 May 2016, effective 12 May 2016, "after service of this order upon his solicitors" (Woodfines), the Judge's mea culpa agreed "this claim was correctly brought by way of a judicial review". Mr Bowers was granted 14 days in which to renew his application, that is, on or before 26 May 2016. Two important words had been overlooked by you and GLD - "costs reserved".

Mr Bowers spent the first week attempting to confirm he wanted Ms Sandbach to proceed and confirm to the Court his original intention to go to judicial review. He was assured on a daily basis that Ms Sandbach would return his calls but she never did. It is assumed she had already left the employment of Woodfines for her new post in Luton.

When Keith Jones sought to achieve accommodation with HMCTS, the date was 26 May, the fourteenth day. In that email he said Woodfines had never put themselves on the Court record despite an exchange of letters between Woodfines and the Court. You admitted you had sent Mr Bowers a notice of acting in person for him to complete and return. Mr Bowers sent the document to the Court, copied to Woodfines, on 25 May 2016 but expressly declared he did not wish Woodfines to represent him. Why had you done this? You told HMCTS: "It would be an unnecessary breach of confidence to explain why at this stage"! You concluded your email to the High Court with the following ingratiating words: "If the court feels able to declare of its own motion that we are not the claimant's solicitors on the record that would be very helpful in all the circumstances". It would avoid the embarrassment of explaining how and why you had missed the Judge's deadline.

Mr Bowers' assessment was that if he were to delay any longer from taking unilateral action, the opportunity would be lost; he had to take charge. Both HMCTS and the Parliamentary Ombudsman agree he set his intentions directly before HMCTS in an email they received on 24 May - the twelfth day. The Administrative Court Office's email to your Catherine Sandbach dated 26 May 2016 reminded the solicitors Mr Bowers' correspondence in future should be sent via his instructed representatives as opposed from him directly. HMCTS' Redgrave and GLD's John-Charles were found to have either wrongfully intervened or failed to intervene in the due process. There was a colleague, an Inspector, to protect from appearance before a Judicial Review.

Permit me now to return to the opening sentence: "We cannot ask the court to waive a fee which is legally payable because you disagree with a judge". How can a fee arise in a case where the Judge admits it was she who was at fault? In what manner did Mr Bowers disagree with the Judge? I suspect you are not au fait with the nuances of this case.

It is unwise to threaten members of the public. I have in mind the last sentence in the referenced letter: "If we hear nothing further by Monday 10 April 2017, we shall continue with the proceedings in respect of our unpaid costs". I seem to remember your claim for bogus costs was heard at Bedford County Court on 14 February 2017. I recall judgement being set aside, the writ cancelled, and costs denied. There was also the revelation you had the impertinence to have a restriction order placed on Mr Bowers' property at the Land Registry. What do you think you are doing? You were representing an elderly man who has had his private property filched. Now we find his solicitor making a move on his home. You are invited to explain to Mr Bowers the nature and origin of your present "unpaid costs". Does your professional body support your behaviour?

1 see here an absolute failure in your duty of care. To ignore a judge's provision, to have no one willing to receive clients' instructions, is not how civilised solicitors behave. If there had been someone available to receive and set down Mr Bowers' wishes on your official paper, we are unlikely to have had the present problem with

uncompliant public servants. Mr Bowers has been fighting his case for over 25 years, in which time he has lost his entire life savings. He relied upon you. You let him down. You can argue that you were not on the record. You provide your own corollary to such a status where the court deals with you as if you are, "and we fully appreciate that in many cases it is expedient and entirely proper to do so". The least you can do now is to contact the case progression official in the Administrative Court office, tell her what has happened and have this case restored to where it rightfully belongs.

Mr Bowers put down five questions for considered replies, together with a supplementary question:

- We had a 'no win, no fee arrangement'. How did the creative accounting figure of £7053.57 arise?
- What was the rationale for the involvement of Courts in Salford and Oldham?
- How do you account for your failure to support me?
- How do you propose to have a Judicial Review reinstated in the public interest and me compensated for the distress caused?
- Why did you find it necessary, unbeknown to me, to involve the Land Registry and my home?
- Are you familiar with the Mear case?

Yours sincerely,

Richard Connaughton

Richard Connaughton

I received a discharge Order 7th. April 2017 from Salford Court (Dep. Judge Thexton) dated 6th. April 2017.

I received an E.mail from Woodfines 13th. April 2017 attaching a statement of accounts. They are still reluctant to answer any questions. I agreed to a meeting with them.

I received an E.mail from Woodfines 18th. April 2017 stating that, because I had referred my case to the Legal Ombudsman, they assumed I did not wish to meet with them. I responded stating that I am still prepared to meet with them subject to the conditions I had previously stated.

I received a phone call at 3.45pm 26th. April 2017 from Susan Parton (Legal Ombudsman). She informed me that she had been assigned to investigate my case **CMP046872. NOTE:** I informed her that I intended to inform the Newspapers about my dealings with Woodfines. She advised me not to contact newspapers until investigations had taken place. I received a letter from Susan Parton (Legal Ombudsman) 27th. April 2017. She requested further information which should be provided by 17th. May 2017.

NOTE!

Because of the complexity of my case, I had to refer to my very extensive file to prepare a summary of events to be considered by the Legal Ombudsman.

I wrote to Susan Parton 1st. May 2017 and enclosed an extensive file regarding Woodfines.

I wrote to Susan Parton again 20th. May 2017 and enclosed a letter written to Woodfines by Mr. Richard Connaughton. I also enclosed a letter I had written to Parliamentary Ombudsman concerning my experience while attending the Royal Courts of Justice. (RCJ), The reason for my visiting the RCJ. was a direct result of the incompetence and maladministration of Woodfines. Because of the actions/non-actions of Woodfines I had been subjected too much distress and financial burden over the past year.

I received an E.mail from Susan Parton 10th. July 2017 informing me that she had received information from Woodfines and is currently finalising her preliminary decision and hoped to inform me within next two weeks,

I received a letter from Susan Parton dated 21st. July 2017 giving her Preliminary Decision on **Case: CMP-046872.** Regarding Woodfines (Solicitors). It was in the usual negative form one expects from Ombudsman.

I received a message from Susan Parton 31st. July 2017 requesting a response to her E.mail dated 21st July 2017. I responded 1st. August 2017.

I sent a letter to Susan Parton dated 4th. August 2017 stating that I did not accept her decision sent 21st. July 2017 and giving reasons why, and enclosing various documents to support my feelings.

I received a response from Susan Parton 7th. August 2017 stating, she had passed my comments onto the Ombudsman, and I should hear within ten weeks,

I sent a copy of a document called "J'accuse II" and covering letter to Susan Parton, 14th. August 2017. The document is an informative and accurate report of the Malfeasance within certain bodies while I was trying to obtain "Justice". She responded 29th. August 2017 acknowledging receipt of documents.

I sent a letter to Susan Parton 19th. November 2017 informing her of much opposition I had received from various bodies in an attempt to pervert the Course of Justice. In the form of **Lies** and **Maladministration** in an attempt to prevent me obtaining "Justice". I received an acknowledgement to my letter 23rd. November 2017

I sent an E.mail to Susan Parton 16th. January 2018 and left voicemail requesting an update on my **Case: CMP-046872.**I received a response later that day informing me that I should have a decision within next 4 weeks.

I received an E.mail from Jason Chapman (Legal Ombudsman) 1st. February 2017 informing me that he had seen the report sent to me by Susan Parton.

He states *"I have come to a significantly different conclusion from the one set out in the report". I therefore want to give you and the service provider an opportunity to comment on the attached provisional decision before it becomes final". Please respond in writing by 15th. February 2018 with any comments on this provisional decision"*

I received an E.mail from Susan Parton 7th. February 2018 reminding me to respond by 15th. February 2018.1 responded 8th. February 2018 stating that I had drafted a response and would send the final copy by recorded delivery within 2 days.

I sent my lengthy response to Jason Chapman (Legal Ombudsman) 8th. February 2018 (sent recorded delivery).

I received an E.mail from Susan Parton 15th February 2018 acknowledging my letter dated 8th. February 2018. She states that because I do not accept the Ombudsman Provisional Decision the case had been passed back to the Ombudsman for consideration, and it is hoped to be finalised within the next 10 weeks.

I received an E.mail. from Jason Chapman 28th, March 2018 with an attached letter dated 27th. March 2018. The letter was 5 pages long. It basically stated that the service I had received from Woodfines failed to provide a reasonable level of service and identified specified items of the service/non-service they provided. They did not consider the actions of Woodfines regarding the Court Hearing "Shortest Court Hearing". To be wrong. They state **"I *note and accept that this happened, but, I do not consider this to be material to the complaints by Mr. Bowers"*.** The letter also states that *"I am not persuaded, as Mr. Bowers has claimed, that the fact that the Judge set the order aside, or that they wrote to the Administrative Court in what Mr. Bowers has described as "Grovelling Communication" is proof that the firm failed to* *provide duty of care to him during the period that they acted or that there was misconduct on their part"* **It should be noted.** The Judge made his decision because, Woodfines attended the court earlier and withdrew they claim.

It is said that Ombudsman are *"Like Tigers without teeth".* I must agree, that is a fair description of my dealings with all Ombudsman I have had the misfortune to deal with.

I E.mailed Mr. Chapman (Legal Ombudsman) 4th. April 2018 explaining that I had recently moved house and had been without telephone and internet for 2 weeks; and would respond to his letter as soon as possible.

I received an E.mail from Legal Ombudsman 9th April 2018 stating I had one day to respond to their request 28/3/2018.

I responded the same day explaining that I had not had a response to my E.mail dated 4th. April 2018; and stated I disputed the Ombudsman's report, and would respond as soon as possible,

I sent a letter to Mr. Chapman (Legal Ombudsman) 12th. April 2018. (special delivery). I gave my reasons for disputing the decision they had made.

I sent an E.mail to Mr. Chapman 30th. April 2018 requesting a response to my letter dated 12th. April 2018.

I received an E.mail from Bride Scully (General Enquires Team Legal Ombudsman) 14:19 1st. May 2018 stating *"Mr. Chapman has now considered your comments but has nothing to add to his final decision "* She also added *"Please let us know in writing, by the close of business today (midnight) whether you accept or reject it. We will then have to close the matter as an assumed rejection, if we do not hear from you"*

NOTE! They sometimes take 10 weeks to respond; and they want me to respond in writing, within 9 hours.

I phoned Ms. Scully immediately. She was very pleasant but had been instructed by Mr. Chapman. Who, had neither the will or courage to inform me himself?

I sent an Email to Ms. Scully 1st. May 2018 stating: *Thank you for your patience in talking to me on the phone this afternoon. You were very pleasant, but unfortunately you have to deliver messages which Mr. Chapman has neither the will or the courage to carry out himself. I totally reject his decision regarding the actions of Woodfines Solicitors. I realise this is the outcome you have always required. However, I will pursue by other means".*

CONCLUSION:

Ombudsman are there to be seen to distribute "Justice". However, they are   very cautious and well skilled in ensuring that certain Authorities, Business's   and prominent people are not exposed for the wrong's they do.

FOOTNOTE:

It is hoped that some courageous and honest person is prepared to place their head above the parapet and investigate the obvious Malfeasance within parts of our society. Alan Bowers.

E.mail: bowers-alan@sky.com

CHAPTER II

A BRIEFING OF THE ACTIONS AND CONDUCT OF
CATHERINE ANN SANDBACH (SOLICITOR) **AND**
HER EMPLOYER *WOODFINES SOLICITOR (BEDFORD)*
JUL Y 2014 -MAY 2016.

It has been discovered by investigation; that, the service and treatment of Mr. Alan Bowers by WOODFINES SOLICITORS OBEDFORD) during the period July 2014-May 2016 was unacceptable and unprofessional.

It has also been revealed that other clients of WOODFINES SOLICITOR (BEDFORD) also received similar service/treatment during the same period. The Solicitor involved was CATHERINE ANN SANDBACH and Senior partner Mr. KEITH JONES.

Although their conduct was reported to The Legal Ombudsman and much evidence was supplied over a long period, it resulted in an ambiguous and bias decision. The Ombudsman agreed Mr. Bowers had been poorly treated. After sometime The Legal Ombudsman gave an unacceptable decision, and stated they would not pursue the case further and would not accept any further discussion regarding the matter.

It has been revealed that action was taken by **"Solicitors Disciplinary Tribunal"** concerning some clients of WOODFINES SOLICITORS (BEDFORD).

The result of the action taken resulted in CATHERINE ANN SANDBACH being "Struck of the Roll" and fined £2600 costs.

This document reveals and indicates the wrong doings and unacceptable treatment supplied by WOODFINES SOLICITORS (BEDFORD).

The Law Society

Dishonest solicitor misled clients about case progress to 'buy time'

By John Hyde | 12 February 2020

solicitor who repeatedly misled clients - claiming she wanted to buy herself time to deal with a busy workload - has been struck off the roll.

Catherine Sandbach was found to have told 'mistruths' on three separate matters to conceal her own inaction, providing them with false reassurances about progress on their cases.

Sandbach, admitted in 2009, had already said she was leaving the profession for good, and she was banned by the Solicitors Disciplinary Tribunal following a regulatory settlement agreement between herself and the SRA.

The tribunal heard that Sandbach admitted dishonesty in relation to all three matters. She told one client a boundary dispute was progressing through the court when she knew court proceedings had not been issued. She did the same - this time over a period of nine months - with a client in a business dispute matter. Sandbach also acted for a client on an annulment of a bankruptcy order and admitted fabricating and backdating an email purportedly sent to the Insolvency Service in order to mislead him into believing she had acted on his instructions.

Sandbach's misconduct took place while she was a solicitor in the litigation department in the Bedford office of Woodfines Solicitors. She was dismissed in 2016.

In mitigation, which was not endorsed by the SRA, Sandbach said she was under a great deal of stress and claimed to have a 'significant' workload, with limited resources offered by her employer. She said she was expected by the firm to deal with matters beyond her experience as a solicitor, which exacerbated her stress. She produced a medical report saying her conduct was influenced by work-related stress which brought on symptoms of anxiety and depression. She was sorry for the difficulties faced by clients as a result of her behaviour and made no personal gain from what she did, claiming her actions were 'simply to buy herself more time to deal with her ever-increasing workload'.

In a statement, the firm said it had not previously seen Sandbach's allegations and it believed she had been treated fairly at all times. The firm 'refuted her allegations' and pointed out that the SRA found no evidence to suggest it acted inappropriately in any way.

A spokesman added the firm has a reputation for being a friendly place to work, with a supportive culture.

Sandbach was ordered to pay £2,600 costs.

[Print this page]

Catherine Ann Sandbach
Solicitor
431024

Prosecution Date: 14 January 2020

Decision - Prosecution

Outcome: Solicitors Disciplinary Tribunal order

Outcome date: 14 January 2020

Published date: 15 January 2020

Firm details

No detail provided:

Outcome details

This outcome was reached by SRA decision.

Reasons/basis

Outcome of SDT Hearing

This notification relates to a Decision to prosecute before the Solicitors Disciplinary Tribunal. This is an independent Tribunal which reaches its own decision after considering all the evidence, including any evidence put forward by the Respondent. The Tribunal had certified that there was a case to answer.

On 14 January 2020, the SDT considered and approved an Agreed Outcome.

Ms Sandbach was Struck Off the Roll.

The SDT judgment will be available at www.solicitorstribunal.org.uk *[link: http://www. solicitorstribunal. org. uk]*

Search again *pink: http://www.sra.org.uk/consumers/solicitor-check/]*

105

SOLICITORS DISCIPLINARY TRIBUNAL

IN THE MATTER OF THE SOLICITORS ACT 1974   Case No. 12016-2019

BETWEEN:

SOLICITORS REGULATION AUTHORITY   Applicant

and

CATHERINE ANN SANDBACH   Respondent

Before:

Mr J. A. Astle (in the chair)
Mr W. Ellerton
Mrs S. Gordon

Date of Hearing: 14 January 2020

Appearances

There were no appearances as the matter was dealt with on the papers.

JUDGMENT ON AN AGREED OUTCOME

Allegations

1.	The Allegations against the Respondent, a solicitor and formerly an assistant solicitor	in the litigation department at Woodfines Solicitors LLP ("the firm"), made by the Applicant were that she:

1.1	Between 1 February 2016 and 31 May 2016, deliberately misled her client Ms SD in relation to her boundary dispute matter by causing Ms SD to believe that her matter was progressing through the Court when she knew that Court proceedings had not been issued, thereby breaching all or alternatively any of Principles 2,4, 5 and 6 of the SRA Principles 2011 and failing to achieve Outcomes 1.1 and 1.5 of the SRA Code of Conduct 2011.

1.2	Between 1 August 2015 and 31 May 2016, deliberately misled her client Mr TM in relation to his business dispute matter by causing Mr TM to believe that his matter was progressing through the Court when she knew that Court proceedings had not been issued, thereby breaching all or alternatively any of Principles 2,4, 5 and 6 of the SRA Principles 2011 and failing to achieve Outcomes 1.1 and 1.5 of the SRA Code of Conduct 2011.

1.3	On or around 14 December 2015, whilst acting for Mr SJ on an annulment of a bankruptcy order matter, fabricated and backdated an e-mail (dated 30 November 2015 and timed at 15:12) purportedly sent to the Insolvency Sei-vice in order to mislead her client Mr SJ into believing that she had acted on his instructions and issued the annulment application by the 30 November 2015 deadline when she knew that was not true as she had not issued the annulment application, thereby breaching all or alternatively any of Principles 2, 4, 5 and 6 of the SRA Principles 2011 and failing to achieve Outcomes 1.1, 1.2 and 1.5 of the SRA Code of Conduct 2011.

In addition, Allegations 1.1, 1.2 and 1.3 inclusive were advanced on the basis that the Respondent's conduct was dishonest. Dishonesty was alleged as an aggravating feature of the Respondent's misconduct but was not an essential ingredient in proving the Allegations.

Factual Background

2.	The Respondent was admitted to the Roll of Solicitors on 15 September 2009. At the time of the Rule 5 statement the Respondent did not hold a current practising certificate. At the material time she was working as an assistant solicitor in the litigation department at the firm, the address of which is: 16 St Cuthbert's Street, Bedford, MK40 3JG.

Application for the matter to be resolved by way of Agreed Outcome

3.	The parties invited the Tribunal to deal with the Allegations against the Respondent in accordance with the Statement of Agreed Facts and Outcome dated 10 January 2020 annexed to this Judgment ("the Agreed Outcome"). The parties submitted that the outcome proposed was consistent with the Tribunal's Guidance Note on Sanctions.

4.   In the Agreed Outcome the Respondent admitted all the Allegations against her including the allegation of dishonesty. The agreed sanction was that she be struck-off the Roll and it was further agreed that she pay costs in the sum of £2,600.

Findings of Fact and Law

5.   The Applicant was required to prove the allegations beyond reasonable doubt. The Tribunal had due regard to the Respondent's rights to a fair trial and to respect for her private and family life under Articles 6 and 8 of the European Convention for the Protection of Human Rights and Fundamental Freedoms.

6.   The Tribunal reviewed all the material before it and was satisfied beyond reasonable doubt that the Respondent's admissions were properly made.

7.   The Tribunal considered the Guidance Note on Sanction (November 2019). In doing so the Tribunal assessed the culpability and harm identified together with the aggravating and mitigating factors that existed.

8.   The Tribunal noted that this was a case involving significant dishonesty. It was repeated across several clients over a period of time. The Tribunal agreed that the appropriate sanction was a strike-off on the basis that no lesser sanction was justified given the severity of the misconduct. The Tribunal then considered whether there were any exceptional circumstances such that would justify a lesser sanction than a strike-off. There were no such circumstances advanced and the Tribunal did not identify any based on the material before it. It was a sad case but one that could only result in the Respondent being struck-off the Roll. The Tribunal therefore approved the Agreed Outcome.

Costs

9.   The Tribunal was content with the level of costs agreed between the parties.

Statement of Full Order

10.   The Tribunal Ordered that the Respondent, CATHERINE ANN SANDBACH, solicitor, be STRUCK OFF the Roll of Solicitors and it further Ordered that she do pay the costs of and incidental to this application and enquiry fixed in the sum of £2,600.00.

Dated this 23rd day of January 2020
On behalf of the Tribunal

J. A. Astle
Chairman

DETAILS OF SOLICITORS DISCIPLINARY TRIBUNAL

Case Number 12016-2019

ARE AVAILABLE IF REQUIRED

....

Date of Tribunal 14TH. January 2020

Before

Mr. J.A. Astle (in the chair)

Mr. W. Ellerton

Mrs. S. Gordon

Decision of Tribunal:

The Tribunal ordered that the Respondent, CARTHERINE ANN SANDBACH, (solicitor 431204) be STRUCK OF the Roll of Solicitors and it further Ordered that she do pay the costs of and incidentals to this application and enquiry fixed in the sum of £2,600.00.

CHAPTER: III

MY STRUGGLE FOR JUSTICE

"THE PATH AND I" CONTINUED

After my rejection by "The Legal Ombudsman" 1st. May 2018 regarding investigating the conduct of Woodfines Solicitors I felt defeated in my attempts to obtain "JUSTICE"

However, during the month of February 2020 while searching the internet I discovered very interesting information concerning Woodfines Solicitors (Bedford)

I discovered other clients of Woodfines had also experienced misconduct regarding their dealings with Woodfines at the same time that Woodfines had been acting for me. Three former clients had reported their experiences to "Solicitors Regulation Authority".

The actions of Woodfines had been placed before "Solicitors Disciplinary Tribunal" 14th.January 2020. The findings of the Tribunal resulted in Ms. Catherine Ann Sandbach being "STRUCK OF THE ROLLS" for misconduct and dishonesty.

Catherine Ann Sandbach (Solicitor 431024) was the same solicitor who acted for me from August 2015-May 2016. It was also discovered that Catherine Ann Sandbach was an assistant solicitor under the guidance of Mr. Keith Jones, a senior partner at Woodfines.

I made a request to "Legal Ombudsman" (28th. September 2016.) to investigate the actions and conduct of Woodfines. I supplied many documents and statements to the "Legal Ombudsman". After many months, the Ombudsman stated. I had been poorly treated by Woodfines but they could find no evidence of Misconduct.

On investigating further, I obtained details of "Solicitors Regulation Authority" submission to Solicitors Disciplinary Tribunal dated 14th. January 2020 and the outcome of the proceedings. I also obtained a copy of an article which appeared in the "Law Society Gazette" regarding the dishonesty of Catherine Ann Sandbach.

I also obtained a copy of the whole proceedings of the case submitted to the "Solicitors Disciplinary Tribunal" which included statements by Mr. Keith Jones and other employees of Woodfines.

Having discovered this information I produced a document called "Justice what Justice" including a report upon "Catherine Ann Sandbach and Mr. Keith Jones a partner in Woodfines Solicitors (Bedford).

In view of this newly found evidence, I wrote to the "Legal Ombudsman" 18th. March 2020 asking them to review my case. The letter was sent recorded delivery, I also enclosed two documents "Justice what Justice" and a report concerning Catherine Ann Sandbach (Solicitor 431024). I also wrote to Sarah Craddock (Legal secretary) Woodfines, informing her of my actions and requested that all the evidence I had supplied be returned to me.

Having had no acknowledgement or response from Legal Ombudsman, I telephoned them 2nd. April 2020 at 9.27am and spoke to a lady called Ron. I also sent E.mail

Details of E.mail & call

Complaint

From: Alan Bowers (bowers-alan@sky.com)
To: inquires@legalombudsman.org.uk
Date: Thursday, 2 April 2020, 09:42 BST

To whom it may concern.
I wrote to the Legal Ombudsman 18th. March 2010 regarding an old complaint No,CMP-046872, I also enclosed 2 documents for your informaion. Because I have not received any acknowledgement or response, I telephoned you 9.27am. 2nd. April 2020 and spoke to a lady called Ron. She informed me that my request had been received and I should have a response within 4 weeks. She also informed me that if I sent in by Email. I would have an immediate response. Therefore I would be grateful fo any information. I reaise these are very difficult times, however, please acknowledge my request.
Please see attached copy of my letter dated 18th. March 2020.
Regards
Alan Bowers

I also telephoned WOODFINES 9.27am. 2nd. April 2020 and requested to speak with Sarah Craddock and was informed she was working from home and I should send her an E.mail. Details of E.mail below

letter dated 20th. March 2020

From: Alan Bowers (bowers-alan@sky.com)
To: scraddock@woodfines.co.uk
Date: Wednesday, 1 April 2020, 17:30 BST

Dear Ms. Craddock.

I sent you a letter dated 20th. March 2020. (Recorded delivery) Received and signed for 6.18am. next day. To date I have had no acknowledgement or response, (copy of letter attached). I realise these are very difficult times.
However, I would be grateful for a response as soon as possible. Regards
Alan Bowers

C CF_000070.pdf 740kB

I received a letter by E.mail 2nd. April from Andrew Carter (Milton Keynes office). The E.mail stated that the complaint had been determined by the "Legal Ombudsman" and they have no obligation to comment further. The letter also informed me that they will continue to retain all my documents, see copy of letter

Our Ref: AXC/CH/BO/083499-001
2 April 2020

Dear Mr Bowers

I refer to your letter dated 20 March 2020 to Sarah Craddock at our Bedford office.

Your complaint has been determined by the Legal Ombudsman and we have no obligation to comment any further.

As we have explained previously, and I refer to Mr Jones' letter dated 27 September 2018, we will not send you any papers or allow you to collect them (which in any event is prohibited at this time owing to the COVID-19 crisis) because there are still costs outstanding in respect of our involvement in your case. We therefore continue to retain a lien over your papers.

Yours sincerely

Andrew Carter
^email: acarter@woodfines.co.uk)

The 6th. April 2020,1 sent a letter and copy of "Justice what Justice" to Andrew Carter (Woodfine Milton Keynes Office). The package was sent Recorded Delivery.

I also informed Sarah Craddock (Bedford).
The letter and document was received and signed for by Woodfines Milton Keynes at 9.7am. 7th. April 2020.

I received a letter from Legal Ombudsman dated 6th. April 2020 (no indication who the letter was from and no signature). The letter was in its usual negative form stating that all the new information I had sent to them 18th. March 2020 was not related to my case and they will not be re-opening my case. I telephoned the Legal Ombudsman immediately I received the letter, and was informed there is nothing they could do.

I will of course respond to the letter, but, I am not hopeful of any positive action being taken.

I sent another letter and a document called "My struggle to obtain Jusice" by recorded delivery on Saturday 11th. April 2020 (see copy of letter below) It was posted and recorded at Flitwick Post office at 11.46am Reference No. NV072765860GB.

Alan. J. Bowers
16 Oak Drive, Pulloxhill, Beds. MK45 5EQ
Tel: 01525 795434 Email: bowers-alanCasky.com

9th. April 2020
Legal Ombudsman
PO Box 6806
Wolverhampton
WV1 9WJ

Your Ref. F077238/ CMP-046872

Dear Sir/Madam

Thank you for your letter dated 6th. April 2020. Your letter did not indicate who the letter was from, and had no signature.

The contents of your letter were disappointing but not surprising, I have been dealing with Ombudsman for many years and have discovered they do not tell lies, they just do not tell the truth.

The evidence I have provided to you in the Document "Justice what Justice" which includes details of action taken against Woodfines Solicitors, in general and Ms. Catherine Ann Sandbach and Mr. Keith Jones in particular, cannot be denied.

In your letter to me dated 27th. March 2020 (Copy enclosed) you state (Para.1 1) "_It would be for other clients of the firm to raise complaints if they felt that the firm had provided them with poor service_". You now have proof of Woodfines poor service, including Lies, Deceit, and Dishonesty at the same time the company was acting for me. This proof is in the form of action taken against them by "Solicitors Regulation

Authority" and "Solicitors Disciplinary Tribunal"

However, in typical fashion you have pushed this evidence aside and continue to state Woodfines "as a firm" are not liable for any misconduct. The evidence you have is COGENT and UNDENIABLE.

I therefore hope you will reconsider your position, and act in accordance with the function of your purpose. "Justice being seen to be done".

I have enclosed copies of letters and documents for your consideration.

Yours faithfully,

Alan Bowers.

Enclosed letters: Dated 27th. March 2018, 8th. February 2018, 12th. April 2018, Document: "My Struggle for Justice"

Sent recorded delivery

I tried to track the delivery Thursday 16th. April 2020 but it only revealed that letter was received at Flitwick Post office... no further details. I contacted Legal Ombudsman 9.30am Thursday 16th. April 2020 and was advised that they had not received the documents and was advised to call back Monday 20th. April.
Documents delivered to Legal Ombudsman 4.44am 17th. April 20120 signed by EDM/JOHN
I received a photo-copy response from Ombudsman

dated 29th. April 2020. No name or signature.

Usual negative response, stating; *"Thank you for you letter dated 9th. April 2020. As stated in our letter to you dated 6th. April 2020, we are unable to consider your complaint, any further and we will not be re-opening your case.*

Any further letters will be read and placed on file but may not be responded to.

You may wish to consider seeking independent legal advice and taking your own legal advice going forward".

See copy of letter

As usual it is their policy; if you do not respond, the problem will go away.

www.legalombudsman.org.uk

WV1 9WJ
☎ 0300 555 0333
www.legalombudsman.org.uk

NAT / 00007

Private and Confidential
Mr A Bowers
16 Oak Drive
Pulloxhill
Bedford
MK45 5EQ
United Kingdom

29 April 2020

File reference: F077238

Dear Mr Bowers

Your complaint about WOODFINES LLP

Thank you for your letter dated 09 April 2020.

As stated in our letter dated 06 April 2020, we are unable to consider your complaint any further and we will not be reopening your case.

Any further letters will be read and placed on file but may not be responded to.

You may wish to consider seeking independent legal advice and taking your own legal advice going forward.

Yours sincerely

General Enquiries Team

**Having had no communications from Legal Ombudsman or Woodfines, I decided to write to both 13th. May 2020.
Details are illustrated below'.**

*Alan J. Bowers
16, Oak Drive, Pulloxhill, Beds. MK45 5EQ
Tel. 01525 795434 Email: <u>bowers-alan(asky.com</u>*

13th. May 2020

Att. Andrew Carter
Woodfines
Silbury Court
352 Silbury Boulevard Milton Keynes
MK9 2AF

Your Ref. AXC/CH/BO/083499-001

Dear Mr. Carter

As you have not responded to my letter dated 6th. April 2020 I am assuming that you believe if one ignores an issue it will hopefully go away.

I wish to advise you, that I and others are pursuing the issue and it will NOT go away, and we are in the process of revealing much that is corrupt and improper within various Departments and other Institutions such as yourselves.

You have the opportunity of responding to my requests or totally ignoring them as you have indicated.

We are all living in desperate and worrying times at the moment. I therefore, urge you to consider your, and your companies' situation, in failing to carry out your duty of care.

Keep safe. Yours faithfully,

Alan Bowers

Sent special delivery

Alan J. Bowers
16, Oak Drive, Pulloxhill, Beds, MK45 5EQ
Tel. 01525 795434 Email: bowers-alanfasky. com

13th. May 2020

Legal Ombudsman PO. Box 6806
Wolverhampton WV1 9WJ

Your ref: F077238

Dear Sir/Madam,

I received your letter dated 29th. April 2020, again, no name and no signature. It appears that you are adhering to your usual policy; no one has the will or courage to respond to issues concerning wrong doing. I have discovered over some time that it is the strategy of some Government bodies and departments that if you ignore a problem it will hopefully go away.

I can assure you that this particular problem will <u>NOT</u> go away. You have purposely not carried out your statutory duties to investigate my complaint, regardless of overwhelming evidence. It can only be assumed the reasons are; Possible repercussions; revealing misconduct and malfeasance within Government Departments; and costs being awarded.

I feel it is only fair to inform you that I and others are in the process of revealing of much that is corrupt and improper within various Government Departments and other Institutions such as yourselves.

You have the opportunity of responding to this letter or totally ignoring it as you have indicated.

We are all living in desperate and worrying times at the moment, and I urge you to consider   your situation in failing in your duty.

Keep safe. Yours faithfully,

Alan Bowers.

Sent Special delivery

Alan J. Bowers
16, Oak Drive, Pulloxhill, Beds, MK45 5EQ
Tel, 01525 795434 Email: <u>bowers-alanCasky. com</u>

14th. June 2020
Woodfines Solicitors
!6 St. Cuthberts Street
Bedford
MK40 3JG

Dear Sir/Madam,

I refer to my recent communications to you April and May this year. You have not responded to my letter to Mr. Andrew Carter dated 13th. May 2020, (Enclosed) I therefore assume you are continuing to use your usual strategy of not replying, hoping the problem will go away.

I informed you in my last letter that I, and others are pursuing the matter by producing and publishing documents which reveals the corrupt and improper manner in which your company acted whilst representing me.

I have enclosed a copy of the first document "Is Justice Just A Word" which I have had printed and will be distributed to many people throughout the land.

I intend to make the documents available to many learned people and organisations who should be made aware of the Malfeasance and Maladministration's which exists within certain parts of the JUSTICE system.

Yours faithfully,

A. Bowers
Enclosed: Copy of "Is Justice Just a Word" Letter dated 13th. May 2020 Sent recorded delivery

Monday 29th. June 2020,1 received a large parcel by courier, it contained a letter and 6 files containing copies of documents and other information I had presented to Woodfines over the years. These files were the documents I had requested twice from Woodfines; who had refused to send them to me.

The letter stated, they no longer wished to communicate with me and contained threats if I continued to pursue my "struggle for Justice" regarding their dealings with me.

(copy of letter attached).

Woodfines
SOLICITORS

Silbury Court
352 Silbury Boulevard
Milton Keynes
MK9 2AF

Tel: 01908 202150
Fax: 01908 202152

www.woodfines.co.uk

Mr A Bowers
16 Oak Drive
Pulloxhill
Bedfordshire
MK45 5EQ

Our ref: AXC/SW/Bo/083499-0001

<u>**Sent by DHL courier**</u>

26 June 2020

Dear Mr Bowers

Rights of Way Dispute

I refer to your letter dated 14 June 2020, received on 18 June 2020.

I refer also to your letter dated 13 May 2020.

We have not adopted a strategy at all. You are fully aware of the nationwide restrictions imposed by the Covid-19 Regulations and that your files were stored at an off-site archive facility.

I have now retrieved your files from our archive.

Although I maintain you are not entitled to these documents because you have not paid our invoice, I now enclose the following to bring an end to your unwelcome correspondence:

1.   Yellow file (1) - comprising of the contents of our correspondence and documents files;

2.   Yellow file (2) - comprising of instructions to Counsel, Mr Feldman;

3.   Yellow file (3) - comprising of supplemental papers for Mr Feldman;

4.   Yellow file (4) - comprising of Mr Feldman's Opinion together with instructions to Mr Mould QC;

5.   Green file entitled *"Alan Bowers - Woodfines Solicitors"* - containing various printouts of historic email correspondence and letters together with various bound documents; and

6.   Red file entitled *"Bowers - Books etc."*- comprising of various bound documents and periodicals prepared by you and others.

I have read your essay entitled "Is Justice Just A Word". I pass no judgement on the contents of this document and I recognise you are free to exercise a right to agree or disagree with those in power.

Woodfines
SOLICITORS

However, your right to exercise your freedom of expression is not without boundaries and if you publish any defamatory statements or material about this firm, its members or its employees you can expect to hear further from us.

In all other respects, we intend to have nothing further to do with you or your continuing battle with local government and the judiciary.

Kindly desist from contacting this firm again.

Yours sincerely

Andrew Carter
Partner
Litigation
acarter@woodfines.co.uk

Alan. J. Bowers
16 Oak Drive, Pulloxhill, Beds. MK45 5EQ
Tel: 01525 795434 Email: bowers-alanCasky. com

10th July 2020

Att. Mr. Andrew Carter
Woodfines
Silbury Court
352 Silbury Boulevard
Milton Keynes MK92AF

Your ref: AXC/SW/Bo/083499-0001

Dear Mr. Carter,

Thank you for your very unexpected parcel containing a letter and selected copies of documents. As you appear to be dealing with this case now, I have addressed this to you.

I have now had time to examine the contents of your parcel. I now wish to make the following comments.

- The parcel contained many carefully selected and copied documents; and a threatening letter.

- It is obvious someone has taken a great deal of time to select various documents and make copies; (although, some of them are my original documents I had sent to you.)

- I have examined the documents you have supplied and, have discovered that some important documents have not been included.

I have read your comments in the letter, in which you appear aggrieved by the information contained in my document "Is Justice Just a Word". Everything within my document is true and can be verified by documents in my possession.

I believe it is only fair and proper to inform you that there are other articles being prepared which illustrate the injustice I and others have had to endure over the past years. After they have been approved, they will be printed and circulated.

I contacted your company initially to seek advice on how to take action against Central Bedfordshire Council concerning "Misconduct in Public Office".

I supplied you with much proven and cogent evidence. Your litigation team examined the evidence and indicated that I had a valid case and entered into a "Conditional Fee Agreement" with me.

However, over the following months I was subjected to very poor and unprofessional service. Eventually, I sort the advice of "The Legal Ombudsman".

I was also subjected to court action (which the court rejected). I also discovered you had approached the "Land Registry" to place a holding on my property.

I contacted your company because my property was being threatened by Central Bedfordshire Council, only to find later you did exactly the same.

As I informed you earlier (By ignoring the problem, it will not go away). There is a saying "When in a hole stop digging".

You have never offered any apology to me for the way your company conducted my case; even though the Solicitor (Assistant) who was dealing with my case has been "struck of the rolls" for misconduct and dishonesty whilst acting for other clients at the same time as dealing with me.

In the Statement of agreed facts which took place at the Solicitors Disciplinary Tribunal dated 14th. January 2020 it can be see that my solicitor (Assistant) Catherine Sandbach was being supervised by Keith Jones (Senior partner). Who has conveniently retired?

You have advised me not to contact you or your company. However, this is an ongoing situation which will be pursued regardless.

Yours faithfully,

Alan Bowers.

Sent recorded delivery.

Woodfines
SOLICITORS

Mr A J Bowers
16 Oak Drive
Pulloxhill
Bedfordshire
MK45 5EQ

Silbury Court
352 Silbury Boulevard
Milton Keynes
MK9 2AF

Tel: 01908 202150
Fax: 01908 202152

www.woodfines.co.uk

Our Ref: AXC/CH/BO/083499-001
13 July 2020

By Email Only: bowers-alan@sky.com

Dear Mr Bowers

Rights of Way Dispute

I refer to your letter dated 10 July 2020 received on 13 July 2020.

Thank you for acknowledging safe receipt of the DHL parcel containing your file of correspondence and documents.

I supervised the return of your documents myself, so I am wholly satisfied that you have received everything that you are entitled to under prevailing Law Society guidance. You have also had all of your original documents returned to you.

As such, there are no "missing" documents. The fact that you have not bothered to specify which documents you say are missing from the files reinforces my view that this is a simple fishing expedition and that your only purpose is to invent or seek out errors where there are none.

You misunderstand: I am not concerned or aggrieved by your publication; it is a catalogue of events and subjective opinions which exposes the fulminations of a former client of Woodfines who is at odds with the judicial system because he was unable to prosecute a plausible claim for misconduct in public office.

There has been no error in our advice (which is qualified by Counsel's opinion) and the only finding that the Legal Ombudsman made was that Ms Sandbach had failed to comply with our usually high standard of client care because her client care letter did not contain adequate information about costs and she failed to provide you with an estimate for Counsel's fees. These matters have no bearing on the SDT decision dated 14 January 2020.

Innuendo notwithstanding, Mr Jones' retirement is entirely coincidental.

Whilst you may continue to be disgruntled about a legal remedy which was never within your legitimate grasp, this is your own business and it not something which will occupy the minds of this firm or its members any further.

Woodfines
SOLICITORS

This is the final response you will receive from us. Any further correspondence from you will not be responded to and will be placed directly onto your archived file.

Yours sincerely

Andrew Carter

Andrew Carter
(email: acarter@woodfines.co.uk)

We confirm that our offices are closed until further notice. We continue to be available to service the needs of our clients remotely, and ask that you speak to your usual point of contact to discuss the best way to remain in communication.

All payments should now be made via bank transfer or card payment woodfines.co.uk/make-a-payment/ and we respectfully request that you not send cheques. We wish you and your families well during these unprecedented times.

Alan. J. Bowers
16 Oak Drive, Pulloxhill, Beds, MK45 5EQ
Tel. 01525 795434 E.mail: bowers-alan(askv. com.

16th July 2020

Att. Mr. Andrew Carter
Woodfines
Silbury Court
352 Silbury Boulevard
Milton Keynes
MK9 2AF

Your ref: AXC/CH/BO/083499-001

Dear Mr. Carter,

I have received your very prompt response to my letter dated 10th. July 2020.

I refer to para. 5 of you letter where you state "I am not concerned or aggrieved by your publications". That however, is not the impression given by the tone of your letter dated 26th. June 2020.

I also refer to your comment, para. 8, in which you infer that my case was never within my grasp. It was your company that advised me I had a very strong case; after being investigated by your Litigation Team, and in fact entered into a "Conditional Fee Agreement" because you believed I had a very strong case.

As I informed you, there were certain documents not included in the bundle you sent to me. I also informed you on a previous occasion; I never release any documents/letters etc. without retaining copies of them. I am not prepared to reveal these at the present time.

You have indicated that you do not wish me to communicate with you in the future. Therefore, I will continue my fight for "Justice" in a more indirect fashion.

I have already informed you that more publications are being prepared, one will be printed and published shortly. Another, more comprehensive publication is being prepared, by myself and others, and will be printed and made available to the public.

You and your company have never apologised to me for the appalling service and distress you have caused me, including taking court action against me, and requesting a holding on my property through the Land Registry. Both of which proved nugatory. I have copies of the Judgement issued by the court, and letter from Land Registry

You can be assured; I and others will continue our fight to obtain "Justice" using every means available to us.

Yours faithfully,

Alan Bowers.

Sent recorded delivery.

....

Towards the end of 2020 I wrote a book called "JUSTICE DENIED" which I had printed and published. The book was made available on AMAZON and other book sites.

During the last week of December and Early January 2021 I distributed copies of the book to various people, including Woodfines (Solicitors). The books were contained in a very robust cardboard package.

29th. January 2021, I received an E. Mail from Mr. Carter (Woodfines) which said, *"We received the attached cardboard packet from you today, but the package arrived damaged open and empty of its contents"* There was an attachment showing a photograph of the packet. (No signs of damage). NOTE! This package was sent many weeks ago to Woodfines and many other people.

I contacted Mr. Carter 30th. January 2021, I explained that the package was sent many weeks ago, I also stated, *"The package contained a book and was sent many weeks ago. It was in a secure package which would require considerable force to open it".* I also added, *"If what you say is true; I recommend you make a complaint to Royal Mail". I informed him that I would send him a copy of the missing book and include other newly published books and documents. I assured him that they would be sent securely.* I advised him that the books are available on AMAZON, WATERSTONES, and other well-known book outlets. NOTE! Many other people who I sent copies of the book to, contacted me to say they had received their copies within two days of them being posted; many made very favorable comments on its contents.

One person who had purchased the book from Amazon said they could not believe all the things that had happened and sent me a cheque for £25 to help with expenses. **Another person contacted me and suggested I make a documentary about the whole affair.**

9th. **March 2021, I delivered a sealed package to Woodfines Milton Keynes office. It was received by Susan Lowther who signed to say it had been delivered. The package contained a letter to Mr. Andrew Carter, and two books, "Justice Denied" and "The Path & I". I also included a draft of a book to be printed and published, the book is entitled "Truth Equality Justice". When the book is published it will be made available on Amazon, Waterstones and other book outlets.**

CONCLUSION:

The contents of this document reveal the corruption and maleficence within certain sections of Government Departments and other institutions, throughout the land.

Most of us accept corruption, and unacceptable behavior exists in many parts of the world, but we do not expect to experience it in our own country.

It has been said ""*All that is needed for evil to triumph is for good men and   women to do nothing*". However, we find many law-abiding citizens are subjected to distress and financial burden; because of the actions of a few who appear to derive pleasure out of causing distress to others.

It can be seen from the contents of this document that many Authorities and Organisations are prepared to use any means such as. (Lies, deceit, false statements, destroying of documents) to prevent them from being called to account for their wrong doings.   And, thereby avoiding any repercussions, such as; failure, reputational risks, costs of compensation due,

When an ordinary citizen attempts to challenge the "Establishment" (Government, Local Authorities etc.) they face resistance, by those who do not wish to be exposed for their wrong doings. Their strategy is to ignore the issue   or by imposing costs; by ignoring the issue they hope the problem will go away.

They know most people cannot afford to employ Lawyers, Solicitors etc. to fight their case, and rely upon this to deter them from pursuing their "Struggle for Justice", and thereby avoiding risk of having to pay compensation for the distress they have caused.

As the Legal Ombudsman works with the Ministry of Justice, it can be assumed that it works with the Government and safe guards its interest.

Through my investigations I have found that it would have been better to have sought Justice through the "Solicitors Regulation Authority" who should be independent of Government influence. However, I chose to approach the "Legal Ombudsman" who do not appear to be independent.

Life is a learning curve, and we all learn through our mistakes.

Over the past 29 years I and my family have endured much distress and financial burden; and many have said "Why do you not give up". My answer is; "because I was always taught to respect and accept JUSTICE". **What Justice!**